The Medieval [...]
of Yorkshire
by
Joan and Bill Spence

Foreword by
Cardinal Basil Hume O.S.B.

Drawings by
Judith Gilbert

Calligraphy by
Duncan Spence

Published by Ambo Publications, Helmsley, York.

1

Other illustrations from:

Monasticon Anglicanum by Sir William Dugdale 1673, 1682, 1849 Edition.

The Ruined Abbeys of Yorkshire by W. C. Lefroy, c. 1890.

ISBN   0   906641   00   4   (Card Cover)

ISBN   0   906641   01   2   (Hardback)

Set in 11 point Helvetica Medium.

For

Anne	Geraldine	Judith	Duncan
&	&	&	&
Geoff	Nigel	Chris	Sue

Acknowledgements: The authors and publishers would like to thank all those who have helped in any way towards the production of this book.

4

Foreword by
His Eminence Cardinal Basil Hume O.S.B., M.A., S.T.L.
D.D.(Hon.).

ARCHBISHOP'S HOUSE,

WESTMINSTER, LONDON, SWIP 1QJ

8 July, 1981

Having known and appreciated Joan and Billy Spence for most
of my life, I am pleased to have been invited to contribute
a brief Foreword to their book.

The Spence family has been very much part of the life of
Ampleforth Abbey for many years. The interest of Joan and Billy
in local history is a long standing one, and they have now
turned their attention to the ancient monastic foundations
of the area. They are both well qualified to do so.

This admirable book is the fruit of their enduring interest
in the former abbeys, monasteries and priories situated in the
Yorkshire countryside. It displays, too, their knowledge of
the history of monasticism and of the individual histories of
the twenty medieval monasteries to which they provide a guide.
This section is delightfully illustrated, particularly by Judith
Gilbert's line drawings. Such a lovingly-produced book should
both please and inform the general reader and impress the specialist.

Cardinal G.B. Hume,
Archbishop of Westminster

CONTENTS

THE ORIGINS AND DEVELOPMENT OF
ENGLISH MONASTICISM

Monasticism in the Western World stems from St. Benedict who, seeing the decadence of an immoral and depraved society in Rome in the fifth and sixth centuries, turned more and more to a religious life based on a distance from the centres of population.

This came at a time when the Roman Empire was in the final stages of collapse. Men needed to adjust, to re-think the meaning of life and find a way to combat the forces which threatened to set Europe back into the age of barbarism.

Although St. Benedict did not become directly involved in making changes in the world of his time, his simple life devoted to God, attracted men seeking to reject the materialistic side of life. In so doing he opened the way for a reassessment of life and a renewal. As this spread, life for many took on a new meaning and their everyday lives, based on a love of God, became more purposeful.

St. Benedict founded a number of small monasteries and he himself settled finally at Monte Cassino, eighty miles south of Rome. He achieved no higher position in the Church than that of abbot. He left no monastic order as we know it today. But he did leave what has become known as The Rule of St. Benedict on which practically all Western monastic life has been based ever since.

The Rule is no hard-bound, dogmatic instruction. It is practical advice for all the various monastic activities.

It places the emphasis on a communal life of harmony, lived with a love for fellow men in the spirit of Christ. It demands no physical excesses and allows, within certain limits, a flexibility of interpretation. It is a short simple document, yet it gives wide-reaching wisdom in its direction and guidance for the abbot and his monks.

It is a design for living and can be applied to the everyday life of people outside the monastery.

Although Christianity had come to Britain in the fourth century, during the Roman occupation, it was all but swamped by the invasions of the Angles, Saxons and Jutes. The firm establishment of Christianity only happened in the sixth century.

It came from two sources. Irish monks led by St. Columba, with the tradition of the Celtic Church, came to Scotland's Iona from where St. Aidan brought it to northern England via Lindisfarne. Pope Gregory I sent forty monks led by St. Augustine, Prior of St. Andrew's monastery in Rome, to England where they were welcomed by Ethelbert, King of Kent, and his wife Bertha in 597. Within ten years Kent, Essex, and London recognised Christianity as their official religion. Augustine and his monks established monasteries at Canterbury and Rochester.

Christianity from this source spread northwards gradually but not without a long struggle as it came up against the effects of paganism and indifference. Due largely to the efforts of St. Paulinus, the Christianity brought from Rome by the men who followed the Rule of St. Benedict became established in the north. Here it met the followers of the Celtic Church, who also played an important role in the spread of Christianity. These two branches came into conflict over certain observances but at the Synod of Whitby in 664 the differences were settled, and Christianity in Britain was unified under the leadership of Rome.

Monks were the mainstay of religion in this country and from their monasteries came a raising of the cultural level of the people. They were scholars, theologians, artists, writers and educators, with Bede and Alcuin among their outstanding members.

This blossoming of monasticism and its spreading effects were violently destroyed and set back a hundred years by the Viking and Danish invasions in the ninth century.

Once England had been united under the Saxon kings, the faint glow of Christianity which remained was fanned into brightness largely by the energetic St. Dunstan, abbot of Glastonbury, and later Archbishop of Canterbury, who revived the monastery at Glastonbury under the Rule of St. Benedict in 943.

He, together with St. Ethelwold and St. Oswald, reopened old monasteries and established new ones. Under these three men the revival in England continued to a point where a meeting of the bishops, abbots and abbesses was held at Winchester in 970. Here the Regularis Concordia, a comprehensive code for English monasteries, within the framework of the Rule of St. Benedict, was drawn up. It unified monasticism and brought it into a closer connection with national life.

This was the basis on which expanding monasticism was able to build after the Norman Conquest in 1066.

William the Conqueror not only exerted his authority as king to help this expansion, but he also had a personal interest through which the Church and Monarchy were closely linked. As that Church was associated with Benedictine monasticism it was only natural that William should encourage the Church in England to expand along these lines.

Inevitably there were men following the Rule of St. Benedict who desired and sought a stricter interpretation of the Rule, with the result that other orders came into being.

The desire for a stricter life, especially in the twelfth century, reflected an urge which was sweeping through monks in Western Europe. It was of no detriment to the Church nor a criticism of the Rule of St. Benedict. In fact the result was a wider spread of monasticism.

The main purpose of a monk's life was to serve God through a love of God and a love of his fellow men. Even though monks often chose the seclusion of remote places for their monasteries, they found they were not able to cut themselves off completely from the world.

Being landowners through gifts, they had to use that land, clear forests, drain marshes and put it under cultivation.

Until the Cistercians introduced a system of monastic lay-brothers, only a little of the agricultural work was carried out by the monks themselves. They employed serfs or paid workers or they had tenants. They started orchards and market gardening and, because of the need for wine for divine services and as a drink, they started vineyards, even in England. They became important raisers of cattle and sheep, with the Cistercians bringing important influence to bear on the wool trade through their sheep rearing.

Because they sold goods and stock, surplus to their requirements, and bought things which they could not produce, the monks became involved in commerce which in turn involved them in improvement of communications.

The monasteries were, for a long time, the chief places of learning and almost the only place where books and manuscripts were composed and copied. Learning and advancement of knowledge emanated from the monasteries. Here lived writers and recorders and through all these works they influenced the thoughts of the society of the time.

Art and architecture were influenced by the monks through their beautifully illuminated manuscripts and through the development of their magnificent buildings.

Monks and nuns in their monasteries were a vital part of the medieval world, essential to its well being and development. The steady and ever-flowing growth of the monasteries was drastically and disasterously cut short by the Dissolution of the Monasteries under Henry VIII. Their influence, so important in their own times, however, continued to mould much of man's outlook and his environment throughout the ages.

THE MONASTIC ORDERS FOUND IN MEDIEVAL YORKSHIRE

The Orders of Black Monks

So named because they wore black habits, the Black Monks came directly from the early monks following the Rule of St. Benedict, seeking a life which would take them away from the world. They desired seclusion but within a communal life, sharing their meditation and prayer with other men searching for a more perfect way of life, devoted to God. But this seclusion did not cut them off completely from the world for they were involved in the life of the Church and their work could take them outside of the monastery.

1. Benedictine

Although St. Benedict (c 480-543) did not found an order it was his Rule which formed the basis of the Benedictine way of life.

Each Benedictine monastery was autonomous. The monks elected their own abbot (or on occasions he was appointed by the local bishop), owed no allegiance to, nor were dependent on a parent house. The government of each monastery rested with the abbot and did not depend upon a central system with a parent house at the apex. The Benedictine system embraced varied aspects of life and the Benedictines became a most influential order, contributing to the religious, cultural, social and economic life of Western Europe.

They came to England through Pope Gregory I who sent St. Augustine to England in 597. The first monastery was established at Canterbury. The order spread quickly but the Danish invasions wiped out monasticism in most parts of the country and it was not revived until the second half of the tenth century. Its full flowering came after the Norman Conquest in 1066.

At the Dissolution there were 282 houses of monks and 92 of nuns.

2. Cluniac

Seeking a stricter way of life under the Rule of St. Benedict some monks established a monastery at Cluny in Burgundy under the patronage of William the Pious, Duke of Aquitaine in 910. The order had a strong following on the Continent until a decline set in after 1048.

The monks did not cut themselves off from the outside world and they used the wealth which came their way for the glorification of God and for the benefit of their fellow men. Their churches were built with great splendour and with a great deal of decoration. The monks attended to the needs of the poor and of pilgrims.

While following closely the life led by the Benedictines the Cluniacs were not self-governing within each monastery. Their priories were subject to the Abbot of Cluny.

The first Cluniac priory to be established in England was at Lewes in 1077. The order never attracted a big following in this country and at the Dissolution there were 32 Cluniac monasteries in England.

3. Augustinian

Often referred to as Austin Canons, the order based its rule on a letter written by St. Augustine of Hippo in North Africa (354-430).

The early history is somewhat obscure. There were canons (clerks) following the rule while administering to the needs of large churches and cathedrals. The Lateran Council of 1059 urged the canons to organise themselves into communities which followed the monastic way of life. Those who did so became known as Canons Regular, while those who did not were known as Canons Secular.

Along with St. Augustine's points they adapted some of the Rule of St. Benedict and also took into account the local needs of the particular community. Their rule, while strict in some ways, was less severe in discipline. Thus they were allowed more freedom outside of the monastery. This brought them into closer contact with the laity

12

especially through their administration of parish churches and the running of hospitals.

They wore black tunics and hooded black cloaks and were known as the Black Canons.

The first Augustinians came to England and settled at Colchester between 1093 and 1099. The order spread rapidly and at its height had 218 monasteries in the country. At the Dissolution there were 170.

The Orders of White Monks

These orders came into existence because some men, following the Rule of St. Benedict, desired to interpret the Rule more strictly. They still followed the communal life within a monastery but sought more seclusion from the world. Nor did they follow the autonomy of the Benedictine houses but were ruled through their parent house.

1. Cistercian

The first Cistercian monastery was founded at Citeaux in Burgundy in 1098 by a band of monks wishing to follow a stricter interpretation of the Rule of St. Benedict.

With the growth of the order the autonomous system followed by the Benedictines was dispensed with and all Cistercian legislation was drawn up by a general chapter of abbots meeting at Citeaux.

These monks, who wore white habits, sought the seclusion of wild places and led a simple, austere way of life so that they would have more time for the devotion of God, for work and for the study of the scriptures. Involved liturgy was not for them and services took the simplest form.

Complete isolation was impossible. As grants of undeveloped land increased and it was brought under cultivation so their influence grew. They employed lay-brothers to do manual work both in farming and building. They became great sheep farmers and were important contributors to England's wool trade.

St. Bernard of Clairvaux was largely responsible for the spread of Cistercianism. He sent monks to England and their first house was built at Waverley in Surrey in 1128. After the coming of more monks direct from Clairvaux to Rievaulx the order spread rapidly and when the monasteries were suppressed there were 80 Cistercian houses in England.

2. Carthusian

The Carthusian Order was founded by St. Bruno in 1084 at Grenoble. The Priory of the Grande Chatreuse had a church and a separate cell with small garden attached for each monk. Here he worked and prayed. Even when in contact with his fellow monks in church or in the refectory (used only on Sundays and Feast Days) he maintained a strict silence except at certain allowed times. He followed a strict and austere life within the Rule of St. Benedict.

The first Carthusian monastery in England was founded in 1178 at Witham in Somerset by Henry II as part of his retribution for the murder of St. Thomas Becket in Canterbury Cathedral in 1170.

The monks wore white habits.

3. Grandmontine

Of only three Grandmontine houses to be found in England one was in Yorkshire at Grosmont. Following the instigation of their founder, St. Stephen of Muret (1046-1124), the members of this order followed an extremely austere life. They held no land beyond the confines of their monastery, they were not allowed to eat flesh of any sort and only persons of the highest rank were allowed into the monastery.

4. Savigniac

Founded by Vitalis de Mortain in 1105 in the forest of Savigny in Normandy, the Order, while following the Rule of St. Benedict, imposed a greater severity on its monks through an austere life of strict rules, severe fasting and heavy manual labour.

The first house in England was established at Tulket, near Preston in 1123 but four years later removed to Furness in Cumbria.

The life of the Savigniac Order was short, for in 1147, at the request of Abbot Serlo, abbot of the parent house, it joined the Cistercians.

Other Orders

From the Orders of Black Monks and the Orders of White Monks it was inevitable that there should arise orders which took something from each while maintaining their basic dependence on a communal monastic life of prayer and meditation.

1. Premonstratensian

Several separate orders of Regular Canons came into being. Of these the Premonstratensian was the only one which established itself with any significance in England. St. Norbet founded the order in 1120 at Premontre in France. He modelled it on the Cistercian way of life while following the Augustinian rule and centralised authority on the parent house. The first house in England was founded at Newhouse in Lincolnshire in 1143.

They wore a white habit and were known as the White Canons.

There were 34 monasteries at the Dissolution.

2. Gilbertine

The only monastic order to be founded in England was the Gilbertine. St. Gilbert, a parish priest of Sempringham in Lincolnshire, built a small convent close to his church at the request of seven women in 1131. He added lay-sisters to help with the work inside the convent and later inaugurated lay-brothers to tend to the land. Because of the growth in numbers, St. Gilbert found that it would be necessary to expand. He sought an amalgamation with the Cistercians. At this time the Cistercians were busy absorbing the Order of Savingy and gave no encouragement to St. Gilbert. He was persuaded by Pope Eugenius III to regard his foundation as an order in its own right.

He drew up a code. The nuns followed the Benedictine regulations, the canons the Augustinian rule and the lay-brothers and lay-sisters that of the Cistercians.

Some of the Gilbertine monasteries were double. These were designed in such a way that the only door between the canons' house and the nuns' house was in the presbytery and was only opened on certain ceremonial occasions. The nuns used the northern half of the church, the canons the southern half, with a partition wall between, high enough so that they could not see each other and yet allowing the nuns to hear Mass.

The men wore a black habit and white cloak while the nuns dressed in a black cloak and black tunic with a white cowl.

The order never expanded as did the Benedictine and the Cistercian orders and at the Dissolution there were 24 Gilbertine houses in the country.

The Orders of Friars

The friars, or mendicant brothers, came into being because the developing social conditions in the thirteenth century bred heresy. It seemed desirable to confront this by having men who would go among the laity preaching the truth and confounding the questioners. So the accent of their training and life was the study of theology.

Though strictly not monks they were essential to the life of the growing Church and their houses must be considered for a truer picture of medieval times.

1. Dominican

The order was founded in Spain by St. Dominic of Osma (1170-1221), a member of the Augustinian Order of Canons Regular. Emphasis was placed on intellectual training and education. It seemed natural, therefore, to found the first house at Oxford.

They wore a white tunic and scapular and a black cloak. They became known as the Black Friars.

There were 49 Dominican houses in England at the Dissolution.

2. Franciscan

St. Francis of Assisi (1182-1226), although he had no desire to establish a monastic order based on the precepts of poverty, chastity, and obedience, found that he had many followers. Some of his extreme views led to controversy and after his death the Franciscans followed the example of the Dominicans in their attitude to learning and were soon sending friars among the laity to preach the truth. The first house to be established in England was at Canterbury in 1224, and at the Dissolution there were 64 houses.

3. Augustinian

In 1256, by order of Pope Alexander IV, the fifteen congregations of Augustinian Hermits were united and became the Augustinian Friars. They had come to England in 1248 and established a house at Clare in Suffolk. The order spread quickly and at the Dissolution there were 34 houses in England run by the Augustinian Friars.

4. Crutched

The Friars of the Holy Cross came to England at the beginning of the thirteenth century and established a hospital in Reigate. Though they did not become an important order in England their work was never the less commendable and York felt their influence through their three years' stay in the city. Eleven monasteries came into existence but at the Dissolution there were only five.

The friars wore a brown or black habit with a red cross marked on the front. They also carried a wooden staff on which there was a cross. By the order of Pope Pius II the colour of the habit was changed to blue and a small silver cross replaced the wooden one.

5. Carmelite

The Moslem occupation of Palestine made life unsafe for the Carmelite monks whose order was established about 1154, though it is said that they drew something of their life from the hermits supposedly living on Mount Carmel. Fleeing Palestine, they settled in various places on the Continent and came to England in 1241. Their first settlements were at Hulne in Northumberland and Aylesford in Kent. Their way of life changed and with the relaxing of a very strict observance they began to follow the Dominican ideas. So from being an order whose monks based their lives on their monastery they became an order with a greater emphasis on preaching to the laity.

6. Sack

This small order originated in Italy and founded its first house in England at Aldgate in London. Of their sixteen houses in England one was in York but all had disappeared by 1314. The name Sack came from the fact that their habit was shapeless coarse cloth.

7. Trinitarian

The Friars of the Holy Trinity were formed in Paris at the end of the twelfth century. While following the Rule of St. Augustine they made their main objective the rescue of Christian prisoners in the hands of the Moslems as a result of the Crusades. They paid ransoms and it is said that the release of 90,000 captives was gained this way.

Their first English house was set up in 1224 at Moatenden in Kent. Of the ten houses in England, all of which survived until the Dissolution one was in Yorkshire.

A red and blue cross adorned the front of their white habit while their cloak had two crosses on the left side.

GLOSSARY

KEY

A.	Abbot's Lodging.	Rooms set aside for use by the abbot.
	Aisle.	A section of the church parallel to the choir or nave, and divided from it by an arcade.
	Apse.	A semicircular termination to the chancel, chapel or aisle.
	Arcade.	A row of arches.
	Aumbrey.	A recess in a wall which could serve as a cupboard.
	Bay.	Section of a building between columns or buttresses.
	Buttress.	A projection from a wall to help support particular loads especially side thrusts from roofs.
B.	Cell.	A small room or hut for one person.
C.	Chancel.	Eastern part of the church in which the altar stands.
D.	Chapel.	A small section of the church, or a small building having its own altar.
E.	Chapter-house.	A building attached to the monastery in which the monks met to discuss the affairs of the monastery.
F.	Choir.	Structurally that part of the church in which singers have their place often inaccurately used for eastern arm.
	Claustral buildings.	Pertaining to the cloister.
	Clerestory.	Part of the church wall above the triforium or arcade usually containing windows.
G.	Cloister.	A covered passage around a quadrangle at the side of the church.
	Crossing.	Part of a church where the transepts cross the nave.
	Crypt.	Area underneath a church.

Glossary

	Decorated.	Term applied to style of English Gothic architecture c. 1275-1340, in which there was an increasing use of decoration.
H.	Dorter.	Monastic dormitory.
	Early English.	Term applied to the first part of the Gothic style of architecture which flourished c. 1180-1275.
I.	Frater.	Monastic refectory or dining hall.
	Garderobe.	Individual lavatory or privy.
J.	Gatehouse.	A building at the entrance to the monastic grounds.
K.	Guesthouse.	Buildings set aside for visitors to the monastery.
	Gothic.	A style of architecture which flourished in Western Europe between the twelfth and sixteenth centuries. In England it included Early English, Decorated and Perpendicular styles.
L.	Infirmary.	Hospital.
M.	Infirmary Kitchen.	Kitchen attached to the hospital.
N.	Kitchen.	The room in which the cooking was done. There could be three in a monastery. One attached to the monks frater, one in the abbot's lodging and one attached to the Infirmary.
	Lancet.	Single, slender, tall, pointed window in twelfth and thirteenth century Gothic architecture.
	Lavatory. Lavatorium.	Trough where monks washed hands before meals.
O.	Lay-brothers' dorter.	Dormitory for lay-brothers.

Glossary

P. **Lay-brothers'**
frater. Dining room for lay-brothers.

Lights. A sub division of a multiple window.

Lintel. Horizontal wood or stone over a fireplace, door, etc.

Misericord. Decorated shelf placed on the underside of hinged seat in choir stall, to provide support against which to lean while standing.

Misericorde. Additional monastic refectory in which special food was permitted.

Narthex. Western compartment of church. Vestibule across the west end of the church.

Q. **Nave.** Main body of church, normally west of sanctuary, transept and choir.

Norman. Style of architecture developed by the Normans which flourished in England after the Norman conquest to about 1200.

Perpendicular. Style of English Gothic architecture which flourished in England c. 1350-1550.

Piers. Mass of upright masonry supporting arches, a pillar.

Pinnacle. A small turret at the upward termination of a buttress, wall or roof, etc.

R. **Presbytery.** Part of the church around the high altar to the east of the choir.

S. **Prior's**
Lodging. Rooms set aside for use of the prior.

Range. Block of buildings.

T. **Reredorter.** Annex to monastic dormitory containing garderobes or latrines.

Romanesque. Style of architecture which was prevelant in Western Europe c. 950-

Glossary

		1150. In England it was known as Norman.
	Rose Window.	Circular window with radiating tracery resembling spokes in a wheel.
U.	Sacristy.	Room close to an altar where sacred vessels and vestments were kept.
	Scriptorium.	Room in which scribes did their writing and copying of manuscripts.
	Solar.	Upper living room in a medieval building.
	Squint.	A hole through a pier or wall so that the high altar could be seen from a place where otherwise the view would be blocked.
	String course.	Projecting horizontal length of masonry.
V.	Tower.	A tall structure generally set above the crossing of the church or the west front.
	Tracery.	Decorative open patterns in the stonework at the heads of Gothic windows, etc.
W.	Transept.	Cross arm of a cruciform church, normally running N-S.
	Transitional.	A period of architecture which marked the period between the Norman and Gothic styles when both were intermingling. Late twelfth to early thirteenth centuries.
	Trefoil.	A cusped decoration of three lobes.
	Triforium.	A gallery between the arcade and the clerestory.
	Undercroft.	Basement of a building.
	Vault.	An arched, stone roof.
X.	Warming house.	A communal room in the monastery where a fire was allowed.

Guide to Twenty Monasteries

BOLTON PRIORY

The Priory of St. Mary and St. Cuthbert, set in the beauty of Wharfedale at Bolton, is often referred to wrongly as Bolton Abbey. It was never raised to the status of an abbey and always remained a priory of Augustinian Canons.

The priory suffered badly at the hands of Scottish raiders but from the ruins rose a fine Gothic chancel, the remains of which are seen today.

After the Dissolution a wall was built across the east end of the nave so that it could continue to be used as a parish church. Had the Dissolution not come when it did there would have been a magnificent tower at the west end of the nave. It was begun by Richard Mone in 1520 and if it had been finished would have become an integral part of the church by the removal of the west front.

The building seems out of proportion for the size of the community, which was never more than fifteen. Compared with the usual relationship between church and cloister Bolton's church was bigger both to the west and south, showing that the original church was smaller and that the cloister was never enlarged.

Little of the claustral buildings can be seen above the ground but their foundations can be traced. The octagonal chapter-house was not in its usual position in the east range but was set east of it. The frater in the south range was set on an east-west axis. The parlour and cellar in the west range had the original prior's lodging above them. His lodging was moved to the east range in the fourteenth century. This range also housed the monks' dorter over an undercroft with the reredorter stretching eastwards at the south end of the range.

The monks owed the establishment of their monastery to the de Rumilly family. William Meschin and his wife Cecilia de Rumilly founded a priory at Embsay, four miles to the west of the present site, for Augustinian Canons from Huntingdon in 1120. In 1154 under the patronage of Alice de Rumilly, Cecilia's daughter, they moved to Bolton. The story goes that Alice's son, the boy Egremond, was drowned while trying to cross the River Wharfe at the Strid. In memory of her son she gave land, near the fatal crossing, to the monks to build their priory. It is a story commemorated in a Wordsworth poem.

Forty years after its foundation Bolton Priory became independent of Huntingdon and remained so throughout a fairly uneventful history. Dissolution came in 1540 when it was acquired by the Cavendish family who became Dukes of Devonshire from 1694. They added to the monastic gatehouse, which has some fine vaulting, and which has become Bolton Hall.

BYLAND ABBEY

In 1134, twelve monks of the Order of Savigny left Furness Abbey (Cumbria) to establish a new house at Calder in Cumberland, with Gerald as their abbot. Raiding Scots made life unbearable and demolished their work so, after three years, the monks returned to their parent house.

Because Gerald refused to resign his abbacy and held that his monks should still keep their vow of obedience to him, they were refused admission. Determined to keep their independence, they searched for somewhere to build a monastery. Because of their impoverished state they decided to seek help from Thurstan, Archbishop of York, whom they knew had helped some monks from St. Mary's Abbey, York, six years earlier.

At Thirsk, still twenty miles short of their destination, notice of their plight reached Lady Gundreda, mother of Roger de Mowbray. He, though still under age, would soon inherit vast estates. Her uncle, Robert d'Alney, who had been a monk at Whitby but had left to fulfil his desire to lead a hermit's life, lived at Hood Grange, on the slopes of Hood Hill, close to the foot of Sutton Bank, six miles east of Thirsk. Lady Gundreda prevailed upon him to share his home with the wandering monks until her son became of age and would be able to offer them greater help to build their own monastery.

While at Hood, Abbot Gerald journeyed to Savigny and, in 1142, obtained from the general chapter of the Order release from the authority of Furness. Gerald died at York on his return journey and was buried at Hood. Roger, who was elected abbot, held the position for 54 years.

After four years, Hood was becoming crowded as their numbers had grown, so Roger de Mowbray gave them land close to the present village of Old Byland near Rievaulx Abbey, which had already been established for twelve years. This nearness of the two abbeys was

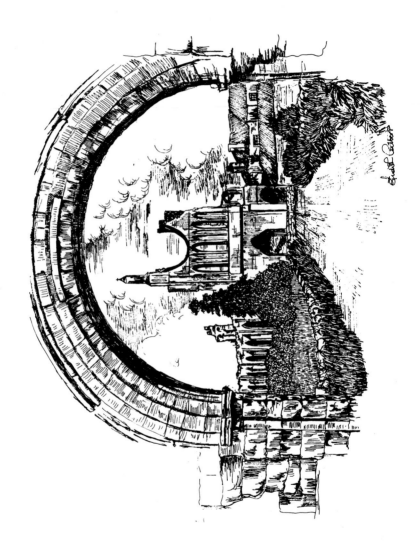

28

disturbing, and the newcomers moved in 1147 to land, once again given by Roger de Mowbray, at Stocking, now the village of Oldstead. While they were here the Abbot of Furness tried to re-establish his authority over them.

In 1147 the Order of Savigny joined the Cistercians and the claims of the Abbot of Furness were referred to Aelred, Abbot of Rievaulx, head of the Cistercian Order in England. His judgement gave the monks at Stocking complete independence from Furness.

During their thirty years at Stocking they built a small church and living quarters but still they were not settled. Roger de Mowbray gave them more land, the present site of Byland Abbey. While still at Stocking they drained the marshy ground, cleared woods and started building their monastery.

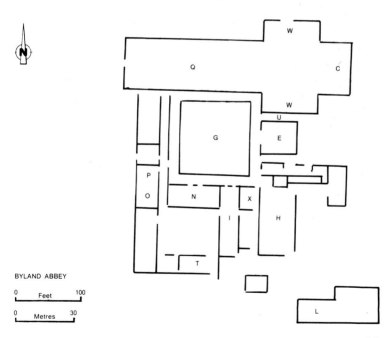

BYLAND ABBEY

0   Feet   100

0   Metres   30

Byland suffered at the hands of the raiding Scots, especially after the Battle of Byland in 1322. Edward II, after an unsuccessful expedition against the Scots, was followed south by Robert Bruce. Unaware that their pursuers were close, the English army camped for the night on Blackhow Moor, on the hills above Byland, and the king sought a night's lodging at the abbey. The Scots, using the protection of the hillside, outflanked the English and inflicted a heavy defeat. When news of the outcome was brought to Edward he fled to the protection of York, leaving the whole of the north of England at the mercy of the Scots.

Little disturbed the peace over the next two hundred years and the monks continued their building, glorifying God with their devotion, and their monastic and social work.

It is a pity that there is not much stonework left at Byland as there is at Rievaulx. The size and magnificence would then have been better appreciated for though the ground plan is clearly visible it does not make the same impact.

It was a large abbey with a church and a cloister bigger than either Fountains or Rievaulx. Byland being built in the 1170's, a later period of Cistercian building, the influence of Burgundian architecture had diminished and the English influence had exerted itself. Here are open transept aisles designed to use vaulting, and the insertion of the triforium bringing the elevation in relation to the ground plan.

The layout follows the Cistercian plan and is similar to that of Rievaulx with small deviations. The infirmary is set to the south-east and not joined to the main buildings, and the chapter-house is the usual Cistercian square plan.

Byland's ruined glory is the west front, simple in style, without towers as was the Cistercian practice, but with what must have been a magnificent rose window 26 feet in diameter. The setting sun streaming through beautiful stained glass must have cast an inspiring and peaceful glow in the church, almost all of which was laid with yellow and green tiles set in geometrical patterns. Some of this work can still be seen in the south transept.

The magnificence of the west front as we see it now would be marred somewhat by a narthex, or west porch, when the abbey was in use. The type which was built at Byland was peculiar to some of the Cistercian houses. This addition of a small porch across the west front, with a roof sloping to the bottom of the west window, was used at Byland, Rievaulx and Fountains and was never developed into a pleasing feature as in the great Benedictine churches. Pilgrims did not arrive in great numbers at the remote Cistercian abbeys so there was no need to develop a large narthex or vestibule in which they could congregate. Their narthexes remained undeveloped as the Cistercians saw no need to incorporate a feature which was not an absolute necessity.

The lay-brothers' quarters, which are larger than those at Rievaulx, are 275 feet long, had two storeys and are older than any of the other monastic buildings. It may be that they were put up first so that the lay-brothers had accommodation while constructing the rest of the abbey, the monks being able to return to Stocking.

As in all Cistercian monasteries, in order to accommodate the monks and lay-brothers with adequate buildings on the east and west sides respectively, the frater was set at right angles to the cloister on the south side. The frater, which usually opened off the cloister at the same level, is in Byland set 5 feet higher, so allowing for a vaulted storage room beneath. The kitchen, which had a central fireplace, was split in the sixteenth century, leaving a small room at the east end enabling two fireplaces to be erected back to back.

The original cloister had open arches on twin shafts, as can be seen at Rievaulx, but it was rebuilt in the fifteenth century with traceried windows set in a wall.

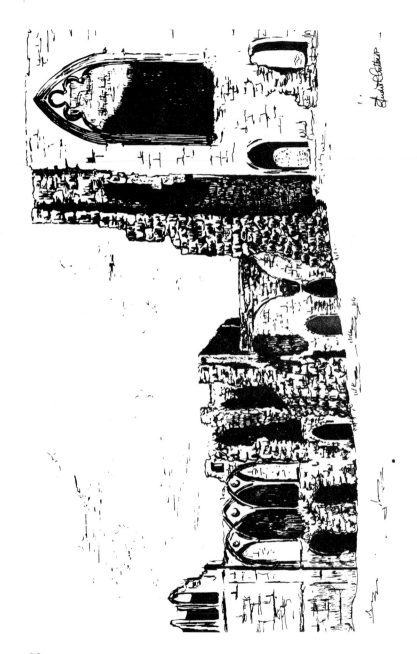

EASBY ABBEY

Easby Abbey lies close to the River Swale about a mile south-east of Richmond.

It owes its existence to Roald, Constable of Richmond who founded the monastery for Premonstratensian Canons in 1151.

The monks at Easby seem to have led a quiet life devoted to God. Their peace in this tranquil spot was shattered on a number of occasions by Scottish raids during the fourteenth century. In 1346 it was used by the English army to billet troops on their way to confront the Scots at Neville's Cross. Unfortunately these men inflicted severe damage on the monastic buildings.

When Richard, Lord Scrope, increased the abbey's endowments in 1392 it enabled the number of Canons to be increased by ten to twenty-nine. At the Dissolution in 1537 there were eighteen canons.

Dedicated to St. Agatha, the abbey is interesting for its layout, particularly in the west range of buildings. These, bordering the cloister which is not of the usual rectangular pattern, are built on sloping ground. This has been used to advantage giving the buildings an unusual character. They are of two sections. That nearest the cloister consisted of four rooms, with dorter over, the most northerly being the warming house. The building to the south of this range and extending across the west end of the frater was also of two storeys, the Prior's solar being over the guest hall. But because of the fall of the land the prior's solar is on the same level as the four rooms to the north which are all on ground level in relation to the cloister. The second range of buildings in the west range consists of the guests' solar and the rere-dorter, flushed by a mill race. This section was of three storeys.

The whole of the west range is extremely functional and ingenious in the use of land affording a layout which housed both the Canons and their guests while keeping them separate. allowing them entry to the reredorter at three different levels and enabling them to reach the cloister through different doorways.

The impressive remains of the frater on the south side of the cloister show a building of large size. The undercroft to the frater is dated early thirteenth century and was vaulted from a central row of octagonal piers. The frater was altered in 1300 and evidence of this work remains in the five-light east window with a narrow lancet flanked by broad lights, the whole topped with a five-trefoiled circular window. The six windows in the south wall were of three lights all with geometrical tracery.

It is a pity that little remains of what must have been a magnificent church but its plan can be clearly traced. The original church was smaller with the present pres-

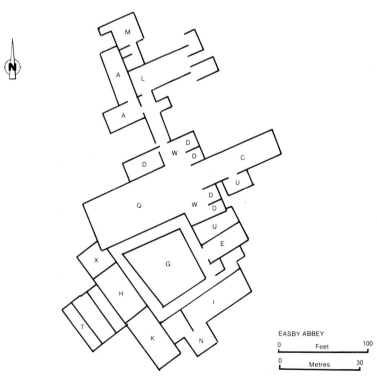

EASBY ABBEY

bytery added about 1340 when the old presbytery became the choir. The chapels in the north and south transepts were not separated from each other but were cross-vaulted as an aisle. It is thought that some of the tomb recesses and graves mark the resting places of members of the Scrope family.

To the north of the church lies the unusual complex of the infirmary buildings and abbot's lodging.

Lying a little way from the main buildings is the gate-house which was rebuilt in the early fourteenth century and remains almost intact.

Between the gate house and the abbey lies the parish church of St. Agatha. Though most of the present building is thirteenth century it is known to have existed before the abbey was built. The font is early Norman, about 1100, and is one of the oldest in the country. There is a copy of the remains of Easby Cross, the original of which dates from the late seventh or early eighth century. Found in 1932, the original remains are in the Victoria and Albert Museum.

After the Dissolution the abbey fell into ruin but the fine canopied stalls with carvings of the breaches of monastic discipline were removed and are in Richmond parish church.

EGGLESTONE ABBEY

From its position on a knoll, a mile out of Barnard Castle, the ruins of the Premonstratensian abbey of Egglestone overlooks a beautiful, tree-lined section of the River Tees.

Dedicated to St. Mary and St. John the Baptist, it was founded in 1195 by Ralph de Multon for monks from Easby Abbey. Never a large community, probably no more than fifteen at its height, the monks were continually beset by poverty. Early in the thirteenth century attempts were made to reduce its status to that of a priory but these were successfully resisted. It suffered terribly at the hands of the Scots in 1323 and the community moved to other monasteries while repairs were carried out. Back in their own monastery the monks were not finished with harrassment, for, in 1346, as the English Army went to meet the Scots in battle at Neville's Cross, the troops created havoc in the abbey. Except for internal upheavals life at Egglestone settled down until dissolution came on 5 January 1540.

The site and buildings were granted to Robert Strelly in 1548. He dismantled the greater part of the church and evidence of his work of converting the east range into a dwelling house can still be seen. Eventually it came into the possession of John Morritt of nearby Rokeby. Abbey buildings became farm labourers' cottages and much of the abbey might have disappeared altogether had it not been for Major H. Morritt. He placed the abbey in the care of the Commissioners of Works in 1925, recovered some of the materials taken from the site and returned them to their rightful place. He also brought back the magnificent, carved tomb of Sir Ralph Bowes from nearby Mortham. It now stands lidless in the crossing of the church.

Close by this tomb are a number of gravestones in good state of preservation, one in particular showing a hand clasping a crozier.

The church, with the remains of what must have been a plain but attractive, unusual mid-thirteenth century five lancet east window, has certain peculiarities which have come about because of rebuilding. The original church was smaller with a south transept and a nave both narrower than those which are evident today. The south transept became broader than the north when it was enlarged in 1275 during the rebuilding of the church in the second half of the thirteenth century. The enlarging of the choir and presbytery resulted in aumbrys being inserted in the east wall and this was used as a sacristy with the altar placed in the second bay.

The north and west walls of the nave are from the original church but the south wall with its fine windows is from the rebuilding period when the nave was widened. The turret, built at the angle of this south wall with the transept, dates from the fifteenth century and contained a staircase. The original doorway in the west front was blocked up when the south wall was built, for a new one was inserted at the west end of the south wall.

The ground plan of the buildings in the north and west ranges can be clearly seen. In the north range the frater was built over the warming house and storage rooms. The small room at the north end of the west range was the kitchen, placed there for easier access to the frater.

The cloister stretches beyond the west end of the church while the claustral buildings are in an unusual position, being on the north side of the church rather than on the south side, in order to take advantage of the better drainage facilities offered by Thorsgill Beck.

There are more remains in the east range because this was the section converted into a dwelling house. Next to the north transept was the chapter-house of which only the foundations remain. The monks' dorter was over the rest of the ground floor rooms. Stretching beyond the north wall of the adjoining north range was the vaulted undercroft of the reredorter with the drain, still well preserved, running along its north wall.

Sir Walter Scott, loving this stretch of the Tees, visited Rokeby on a number of occasions, the first being in 1809. Enchanted by the area he used it for his romantic poem Rokeby, completed in 1812. In it he says of Egglestone Abbey:

> The reverend pile lay wild and waste,
> Profaned, dishonour'd and defaced,
> Through storied lattices no more
> In soften'd light the sunbeams pour,
> Gilding the Gothic sculpture rich
> Of shrine and monument and niche.

40

FOUNTAINS ABBEY

The twelve Benedictine monks who left St. Mary's Abbey, York, and came under the protection of Archbishop Thurstan were taken by him to his estates at Ripon to commemorate Christmas in 1132. While there he made them a grant of some land a few miles away in Skelldale.

Here, under the protection of a large elm tree, they erected their first, simple dwellings. There were ample springs coming from the steep slopes of the valley from which the abbey got its name. Dedicated to Our Lady, the abbey became known as St. Mary of the Springs – Sancta Maria de Fontibus – Fountains.

The early life for the handful of monks was hard and austere in this place which was wild and remote, not at all as it appears today. In those early days the monks depended on Archbishop Thurstan's generosity to keep going.

The prior, Richard, was elected abbot and in 1133 they sought permission from St. Bernard, Abbot of Clairvaux, to join the Cistercian Order. This was given and Geoffrey, a monk at Clairvaux, was sent to instruct the men at Fountains in the rules and regulations appertaining to the Cistercian way of life.

Life remained hard and it looked as if the effort to establish a thriving monastery would fail. Their saviour came in 1135 when Hugh, Dean of York, resigned from his office and joined the monks at Fountains. He had wealth and, as a scholar, books which formed the beginning of a library in his new abode.

Hugh's coming drew attention to the community and it was not long before other benefactors came forward with help. The position changed appreciably and work was begun on more permanent buildings following the usual Cistercian plan. Fountains' reputation spread and men seeking the Cistercian way of life swelled the community numbers to such an extent that the monks were able to carry out one of their functions of running a mission house. Eight new monasteries were established from Fountains.

When William Fitzherbert was elected Archbishop of York in 1141, following the death of the generous Thurstan in the previous year, the Cistercians, suspecting that the election had not been straight-forward and doubting the character of Fitzherbert raised protests. These were maintained until finally, in 1147, the Pope deposed Fitzherbert. Some of his followers, knowing that Abbot Murdac of Fountains had played no small part in the Archbishop's dismissal, attacked Fountains, burnt what they could and left many of the buildings damaged. It is supposed that one of the objects of the attack was to kill Abbot Murdac but he escaped the avengers' swords, "for the hand of the Lord protected him" as he lay prostrate in front of the altar.

Like many of the abbeys in the north, Fountains suffered at the hands of the Scots especially during the routing of Edward II.

In spite of setbacks the abbey continued to grow in size and reputation.

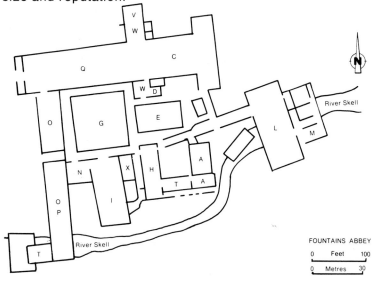

FOUNTAINS ABBEY

0   Feet   100

0   Metres   30

So much of Fountains remains that it is not hard to picture the tranquil lives of the monks in peaceful days in the beautiful setting wrested by them from the disorderly terrain of the Skell valley.

The narrow church extended over 350 ft. Magnificent in itself the aisled nave looks into a chancel which was lengthened from three bays to five in the thirteenth century.

The trefoiled arches and lancet windows surmounting these bays lift the chancel into a soaring lightness. The east end is known as the Chapel of the Nine Altars, a fine feature, which, when it was almost completed, was copied by the builders of Durham who were having to replace some faulty work. To accommodate nine altars the east was given small transepts, an unusual feature in England. This east end with lancet windows on either side of the magnificent central window, delicate slender pillars, marble shafts, a trefoiled arcade behind the nine altars, must have been an unforgettable sight before the abbey was committed to ruin.

The Cistercian plan, following simple lines, precluded a tower so to find such an attractive one at Fountains is unusual. A small tower was erected over the crossing but when Abbot Darnton (1478-1494) tried to heighten it the foundations on the south side were put under too much pressure. Cracks appeared and an extra buttress for the south-east pier can still be seen. However the question of a tower was not allowed to be forgotten and Abbot Huby (1494-1526) was responsible for the erection of a four-storied tower over the north transept.

The west range has a magnificent vaulted cellar erected during the twelfth century. The rounded arches of the northern half indicate the possibility that this section could be of an earlier date, maybe before the burning in 1147. The southern half of this range was used as the lay-brothers' frater and over the whole was their dorter.

As in the Cistercian plan the cloister lay to the south of the nave and gave admission to the kitchen, the frater and warming house on the south. On the east of the cloister was the chapter-house, the entrance to which was through three arches and the inside had vaulted aisles. South of this was the monks' dorter with its undercroft. The range of buildings to the east consisted of the infirmary range the centre of which was the enormous hall carried on four tunnels over the river. The monks made remarkable use of the Skell, channeling it or building over it as dictated by their needs without altering the basic Cistercian plan.

The glory of the abbey in its prime is not difficult to imagine. It is a pity that its magnificence was plucked from it by the Dissolution. Abbot Thirsk, who succeeded Abbot Hugh in 1526, was forced by the King's commissioners to resign in 1536 after charges of sacrilege and theft, in all probability false, were made against him. In 1537 he was arrested for taking part in the Pilgrimage of

Grace and hanged at Tyburn. His successor, Abbot Bradley, and the thirty-one monks surrendered the abbey on 26 November 1539.

The King sold the abbey to Sir Richard Gresham who stripped the buildings of everything of value.

At the end of the sixteenth century it was acquired by Sir Stephen Proctor who took a great deal of the stone to build Fountains Hall. The property passed through a number of owners. Tidying up over the years and the eventual care of the Department of the Environment has saved one of the most outstanding sites in Europe where the layout and detail of a medieval monastery can be studied and enjoyed and where an impression of life in its glorious days can easily be gained.

GUISBOROUGH PRIORY

Though there is some doubt about the exact date of the founding of the Augustinian priory at Guisborough, 1119 is generally accepted.

The land was granted by Robert de Brus, a Yorkshire baron. Among his descendants, buried in the priory church, was Robert de Brus who claimed the Scottish throne in 1291-1292 and who was father of the famous Robert de Brus who became King of Scotland.

Early in the thirteenth century the work of rebuilding the monastery was started and occupied most of the remainder of the century. The Norman church was replaced by a more magnificent building but on 16 May 1289 tragedy struck. A plumber coming down from the roof left his assistants to see to his pan of burning coals. They neglected to do so and as the pan had been placed on dry timber a fire started. Once it took a firm hold there was nothing anyone could do and the result was that it melted the lead roof which flowed like lava from a volcano and engulfed the church, destroying practically all the building and many of the monastic treasures.

A new church was built and, judging from the few remains, this must have been a building to stir the heart. The magnificent east end rises to its full height of 97 ft. The huge east window, flanked by lesser but broad lancets, has lost its stone tracery. It takes little imagination to picture the morning sun pouring in through the east windows to flood the 350 ft. long church with light.

This east end stands sentinel over the few other stones, all that remain of the church and the conventual buildings, a witness to the severe mauling Guisborough priory received after the Dissolution.

JERVAULX ABBEY

A small band of monks of the order of Savigny started a monastery at Fors near Aysgarth on land given by Acarius Fitz Bardolf, Lord of Ravensworth, in 1145. Jurisdiction over them was vested in the Abbot of Byland in 1146. A year later the Order of Savigny joined the Cistercians, so that, when the land at Fors proved unproductive and the site less attractive, it was as Cistercians that the monks moved to a new site at Jervaulx in 1156. The land which was given by Conan, son of Alan, Earl of Richmond, lay five miles north-west of Masham.

Life was peaceful at Jervaulx where, by further grants and diligent work, the monks prospered and their abbey became one of the leading monasteries in York-shire. Money was derived from their sheep farming and from coal and iron mining. It is said that Jervaulx monks were responsible for the recipe for the famous Wensley-dale cheese and that they were well-known for their special breed of hardy horses.

Most of the building was carried out in the second half of the twelfth century. There were some later additions but most of the remains are from the earlier period. It is a pity that Jervaulx suffered so heavily at the hands of the King's commissioners for its church had been described as one of the fairest churches ever seen.

That Jervaulx was destroyed was due to involvement in the revolt against Henry VIII known as The Pilgrimage of Grace. Although the abbot, Adam Sedbergh, tried to avoid implication, he was denounced by a former monk, Ninian Staveley, who, having been involved in the revolt, tried to save himself by turning informer. The abbot was arrested, imprisoned in the Tower of London and put to death at Tyburn. In one of the rooms of the Tower is an inscription, Adam Sedbar Abbas Jarvall 1537. The King's men turned on the abbey, expelled the monks, stripped it of its treasures and blew it up.

The plan of this great abbey followed the usual Cistercian pattern and can be easily traced.

The cloister lies to the south of the nave of the 264 ft. long church. On the east side of the cloister is the chapter-house where some of the octagonal pillars still stand. The long range to the south of this was the dorter over an undercroft which was used by the novices and was later divided into small rooms.

Across the south end of the dorter was the abbot's lodging with a fine, square kitchen with two large fire places.

The west range, following the Cistercian custom, was for the lay-brothers. Their dorter was over an undercroft 200 ft. long, which was divided into their frater and cellars. This is the earliest part of the buildings and no doubt was constructed first so that the lay-brothers had a place to live while they were building the abbey.

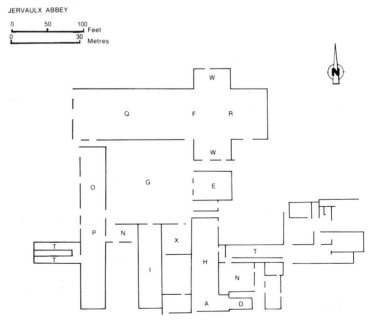

JERVAULX ABBEY

51

KIRKHAM PRIORY

There is no substantial evidence to prove that Kirkham Priory, by the banks of the River Derwent, five miles south west of Malton, owes its existence to a tragic accident, but its story would not be complete without it being told.

Walter Espec, Lord of Helmsley, married Adeline, and they had a son Walter, who liked fast horses and enjoyed hunting. One day, in full chase, his horse stumbled, threw him and he broke his neck. His mother and father were heartbroken and they resolved to found a monastery in commemoration of their son. So Kirkham came into existence, the first of three monasteries which were established due to the generosity of Walter Espec.

Kirkham was an Augustinian house founded about 1125, and the first prior was Walter Espec's uncle, William, who was transferred from Nostell Priory, the first Augustinian priory in England.

Early in its history, negotiation took place for Kirkham to be handed over to the Cistercians of Rievaulx. Some of the Kirkham monks were to join the Cistercians, but those who did not want to do so were to found a new monastery at Linton. A possible explanation for the proposed amalgamation is that Walter Espec had become a Cistercian at Rievaulx (he died there on 15 March 1154) and he may have wished all three monasteries to which he was benefactor to belong to the Cistercian Order. Certain conditions in favour of the Augustinians had to be met, but it seems that these were never fulfilled as the transfer never took place.

Kirkham's later history appears to have been uneventful. It never attained the size nor achieved the reputation of any of its illustrious neighbours, although from 1258 to 1343 it was the burial place for the Lord of Helmsley.

The entrance to the ruins is through what must be one of the finest remains of a monastery gatehouse in the country. A wide, pointed arch gracefully opens the north facade which is enriched with carvings of figures and shields.

In the centre, flanked by geometrical tracery windows, is the seated Christ with St. Phillip and St. Bartholomew in trefoiled niches. The four shields below the top of the gatehouse bear the arms of de Clare, England, de Roos and Vaux. The panelled sills of the windows have shields on either side with the arms of Espec and Fitz-Ralph. The four shields below the windows hold the arms of Scrope, de Roos, de Roos again and de Fortibus. The lower carved figures represent St. George and the dragon and David and Goliath.

The rest of Kirkham's ruins are not in the same grand manner as this ruin of the thirteenth century gatehouse but they are extensive enough to show the full ground plan of the abbey.

The church is long and narrow, the first one being aisleless. Little remains of this building (1140) except the south wall of the nave and parts of the south transept.

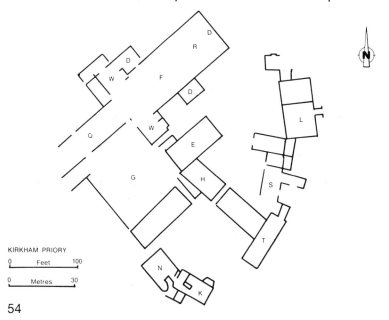

KIRKHAM PRIORY

0   Feet   100

0   Metres   30

54

The remaining walls of the nave and transepts are from the later building (1180). In the early part of the thirteenth century a scheme to rebuild the entire church was started. The choir and presbytery, with aisles, were built. The two western piers were intended to carry a central tower. This was never built, nor were the intended alterations to the rest of the church carried out. So the church remained to the Dissolution a mixture of these three buildings with a small section of the east end remaining as evidence of the magnificence of the thirteenth century building.

Towers were built at the west end at the close of the twelfth century but all that remains is a section of the south west tower, the lower part of which served as an entrance to the cloister.

The cloister lay to the east of the nave and east of this was the frater above a vaulted basement of the thirteenth century. Entrance to the frater was through a finely carved twelfth century doorway, still to be seen. Close to this, on the west wall of the cloister, is a thirteenth century frater lavatory, where the monks washed before entering the frater.

On the north side of the cloister, close to the church was the chapter-house, rebuilt in the thirteenth century. Adjoining this, at a slight angle, was a thirteenth century building, the upper storey of which was the dorter, and at right angles to this, at the east end, stood the rere-dorter.

The ruins to the north of this, curving in towards the church, are those of the Prior's Hall, the kitchen, the misericorde and infirmary with its hall. The guest house with its kitchen lay across the space to the south of the dorter.

These extensive ruins recall, through the imagination, the magnificence of this Augustinian Priory where the monks led a peaceful existence overlooking the River Derwent winding its way through beautiful countryside to join the River Ouse.

56

KIRKSTALL ABBEY

Leeds, within its boundaries, can boast one of the most extensive monastic ruins in the country but unfortunately it has not received the preservation work it merits.

Because a period of poverty during the late thirteenth and early fourteenth centuries prevented new building, it is one of the finest examples of the architecture of the early Cistercian monasteries. It is of severe yet beautiful simplicity. The glory of the rounded arch is self-evident at Kirkstall. Even so there are glimpses of future developments in the architectural world. Pointed arches are being used in the structure and the round, nave piers have attached stonework, forerunners of the piers of clustered shafts of the thirteenth century.

The layout of Kirkstall followed the usual Cistercian pattern and the extent of the remains of the claustral ranges is extensive enough to give visual stimulus to the mind when picturing life in a medieval Cistercian monastery.

The east range consisted of a book-recess, where books to be read in the cloister were kept, the library, the chapter-house, parlour, the day stairs to the dorter which were replaced by new ones at the east end of the south range, and a passage. Over all these was the monks' dorter.

The small chapter-house was extended in 1230 and was entered from the cloister through a double doorway under two beautiful round arches flanked on each side by two smaller arches. The main entrance from the cloister to the parlour was under a single arch, matching the two to the chapter-house, but this was blocked up in the fifteenth century.

The west range, as was usual, was used by the lay-brothers with their dorter over their frater and cellar. The south range held the warming house, the frater, now on a north-south axis replacing an earlier one orientated east-west, and the kitchen.

To the east was the abbot's lodging which, because it dates from the thirteenth century, is one of the earliest examples of separate accommodation for the abbot.

Kirkstall is dominated by the soaring southern wall of the tower at the crossing of the church. The original tower was lower, only reaching to the string-course above the lower windows. The upper portion was a sixteenth century addition and held a steeple which collapsed in 1779.

The community came here from Fountains after a brief sojourn at Barnoldswick. The land there had been given by Henry Lacy, Earl of Lincoln. The site was poor and the monks were continually harrassed by robbers. A move was desirable and they found a benefactor in William de Poiton, one of Henry's vassals. They established themselves at Kirkstall in 1152 and like other Cistercian houses prospered on the sheep they reared for the wool trade.

All was not straight forward, however, and setbacks, probably due to mismanagement, left the monks in such a parlous state that in the late thirteenth century they had to appeal to the King for help. Times took a turn for the better but the ravages of the Black Death and the changed conditions of labour, resulted in a rundown of the community. In 1380 there were seventeen monks and six lay-brothers having once been thirty-six monks and an exceptionally large number of lay-brothers.

The King's commissioners took Kirkstall over in 1540 and, after the valuables had been stripped from the monastery, the site was given to Thomas Cranmer, Archbishop of Canterbury.

Following his burning as a heritic in 1555 there were wranglings about the property until it finally came to the Saville family in 1584. The Earls of Cardigan had it in 1671 and in 1890 Colonel J. T. North, who had amassed a fortune out of nitrates, bought it and presented it to the Corporation of Leeds.

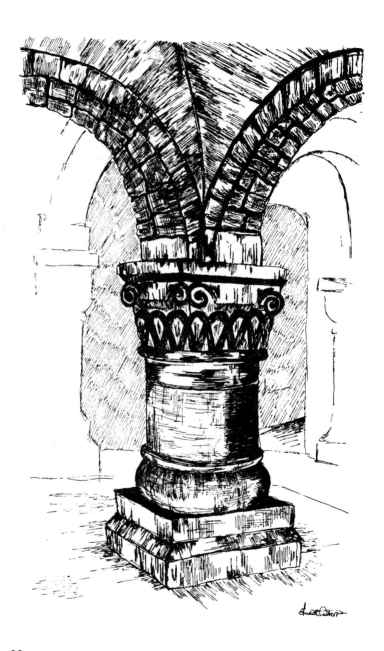

LASTINGHAM ABBEY

Beneath the church in the tiny village of Lastingham, nestling under the southern slopes of the North Yorkshire Moors, is one of the finest Norman crypts in England. It is a complete church in itself, having a chancel, nave and aisles, rare for a crypt in this country.

Hardly touched since it was built in the second half of the eleventh century, this crypt was once part of a Benedictine monastery. But it was not the first monastery on this site. For that we must go back four centuries earlier.

Cedd was a member of the monastery on Lindisfarne, which had been established by St. Aidan in 635. Later he was sent on missionary work to the Middle Angles and East Saxons, but during a return visit to the north, Cedd was asked by Ethelwald, King of Deira, a kingdom corresponding roughly to the old boundaries of Yorkshire, to found a monastery. The king wanted a place to which he could retire for prayer and also a place in which he could be buried.

The king gave Cedd land at Lastingham, which the Venerable Bede, who visited it in 735, described as lying among "mountains, difficult of access and remote, where appeared to be fitter dwelling places for thieves and wild beasts, than for men." In spite of the difficulties of living in such inhospitable country, the monastery thrived for over 200 years.

Cedd and his monks cleared the ground and built a church and a home, probably of clay, wattle and wood. The monks modelled their life on that at Lindisfarne which, because St. Aidan came from the monastery of Iona, was based on the way of life led by the Celtic monks there.

Cedd died of the plague in 664, and the news of his death so saddened the members of the monasteries which he had established among the East Saxons, that thirty of them came to Lastingham to live, so that they could be near their beloved founder and be buried close to him. All except one of them died of the plague. St. Cedd was followed as abbot by his brother St. Chad who later became Bishop of York and Bishop of Lichfield. He built a stone church and re-interred his brother's body beside the high altar.

The Danes, when they ravished this part of the country about 870, destroyed Lastingham so completely that there is no mention of it again until 200 years later. No trace of the monastery was left, and there is no evidence at Lastingham of the burial places of the two men concerned with its foundation, Cedd and Ethelwald.

However, there are two slabs in nearby St. Gregory's Minster, at Kirkdale, reputed to be the gravestones of St. Cedd and King Ethelwald. It may be that hearing of the Danes coming the Lastingham monks fled to the monastery at Kirkdale, taking with them the bodies of their two beloved founders.

Kirkdale was also destroyed by the Danes, and it could be that the attack was so sudden and unexpected that no monk escaped to tell of how St. Cedd and King Ethelwald came to be interred there.

Lastingham next comes into the pages of history in 1078 when, after a dispute, Stephen left the abbey at Whitby, and came to Lastingham to found a monastery, no doubt having heard of its earlier religious connections.

Stephen's monks were continually harrassed by robbers and life became intolerable, so that they decided to move to the protection of York, in 1086. Two years later, aided by William Rufus, they founded St. Mary's Abbey, which was to become one of the foremost Benedictine monasteries in the country.

Considering that Stephen and his monks lived in Lastingham only eight years, building must have been carried out rapidly, for the complete crypt as we see it today was built by them, and above it was the apse and presbytery of the monastic church. This apse and four of

62

the piers remain. There was to be a central tower but it is probable that this and the rest of the church to the west of the present west end was never even begun. No more building was carried out until the thirteenth century after it had become a village church. The presbytery of the monastic church became the nave and the apse became part of the chancel.

Apart from being a complete church in itself, the crypt is also unique as being one of the few in the country to have an apse. The short pillars with heavy bases and capitals support simple round arches. The nave has groined rubble vaulting while the chancel has a simple barrel vault.

There are the remains of Saxon crosses, an old paving slab, or maybe even the altar used by St. Cedd, as well as some ornamental stones which could well have come from the church built by St. Cedd. Whatever the truth of these stones, the crypt has an atmosphere capable of transferring the visitor far back into the past.

MALTON PRIORY

St. Mary's Church, situated in what is now Old Malton, is part of the Gilbertine Priory which was dedicated to St. Mary and founded by Eustace Fitz-John between 1147 and 1154.

The only exclusively English order, the Order of Sempringham, is usually known as the Gilbertine Order after its initiator, St. Gilbert of Sempringham in Lincolnshire. He wanted the Order, which he founded in 1131, to be composed of double houses, that is, one for men and one for women, strictly separated, but within the same precinct.

The claustral buildings for the canons and the nuns were separated by the church, and even within the church, which they shared, they were kept apart by a wall. This was to be high enough to prevent them seeing each other, but not so high as to stop the nuns hearing Mass, which was said at the canons' altar. Of the final total of twenty-six monasteries, twelve were double and the rest, of which St. Mary's Priory was one, were for men only

St. Gilbert took the Rule of St. Benedict, as practised by the Cistercians, for the nuns and the Rule of St. Augustine for the Canons, as well as adapting various aspects of the life followed by other orders to his own.

The canons at Malton were given land from a number of benefactors and much of it was put down to pasture, enabling the monks to derive a great deal of their income from wool. The canons had charge of three houses for feeding the poor in Malton and the neighbouring district.

The dissolution of the Malton Priory was delayed by the influence of Robert Holgate, afterwards Archbishop of York (1545-1554) but the end came in December 1539 when the Prior, John Crawshaw, and his nine canons surrendered. St. Mary's was the last Gilbertine house to do so.

Only the west front, the tower, piers and fragments of the east end remain of the original church, and there are only traces of the other buildings in the neighbourhood. Abbey House to the south of the church has what was the thirteenth century undercroft of the monastic refectory as the basement of an outbuilding.

The church was started about 1150 at the east end, and finished about fifty years later when the west front was completed. The architectural styles move from Norman, through to the fine Early English of the west front. The original church has two west towers, a central tower and was aisled. The central tower was taken down in 1636. In the first half of the eighteenth century the choir was demolished and the nave came under structural alterations, to leave it more or less as it is today. The aisles were removed and walls built along the arcades and across the east end, leaving a rectangular building with the fine arches of the nave and triforium marred by the walls, but still in their entirety.

The clerestory was removed and the roof lowered, which meant that the tracery and upper lights of the fine west front had to be spoiled by being blocked up. Major restoration took place in the second half of the nineteenth century particularly in the roof, which was found to be decaying. It was replaced with an oak roof, based on a fifteenth century design. When the choir stalls were put in, several fifteenth century misericords and bench ends were incorporated.

MONK BRETTON PRIORY

Deep in industrial South Yorkshire, crowded by houses on the west side, stands the ruins of the Cluniac monastery of Monk Bretton. Monks from Pontefract established the priory in 1154 and dedicated it to St. Mary Magdalene under the patronage of Adam Fitzswane.

But all was not straightforward and for over 125 years there were disputes between the two priories, the chief one being which priory should elect the prior of the new foundation. Eventually in 1281 the monks at Monk Bretton broke away from the Cluniac Order and joined the Benedictines and, as was the custom in the Benedictine order, elected their own prior.

An uneventful and peaceful life followed, culminating in the Dissolution when, after the monks left in 1538, one of the King's commissioners, William Blithman, took it over. He sold it to the Earl of Shrewsbury in 1589. The Earl made it a wedding gift to Henry Talbot, his fourth son, who rebuilt the prior's lodging and part of the west and south ranges to use as a residence. It passed through various owners until 1932 when it was bought by the Borough of Barnsley and handed to the care of the Ministry of Works.

Excavations undertaken between 1923 and 1926 produced a comprehensive ground plan.

The broad nave gave into small transepts each with two chapels, and also into a small narrow chancel which, in the fifteenth century, was extended at the east end where a sacristy was added on the south side.

The cloister occupied the south side of the nave. Around it were the usual claustral buildings. The chapter-house adjoined the south transept and next to it was the parlour. A passage ran between the parlour and the warming house with access to them both from the passage and not as usual from the cloister. This east range was topped by the dorter, while beyond it were two separate buildings, the reredorter and the guest house.

On the east side of the south range was a smaller warming house which replaced that in the east range. Apart from this room, the whole of the south range was taken over by the frater so that the kitchen and scullery were situated to the south. The main drain ran through the kitchen yard where an inspection chamber was fitted with a sluice gate.

The west side of the cloister was occupied by cellars over which was built the prior's lodging. The west wall of this has two fine features, a two light window and a fireplace with lintel and lamp brackets, capped by a hood tapering upwards.

To the west of this range are the remains of a twelfth century gatehouse while to the north is the outer gatehouse also of the twelfth century but altered in the fifteenth. It is thought that the building standing on its own to the north of the church was used for administrative purposes.

The infirmary buildings are in their usual position to the east of the east range.

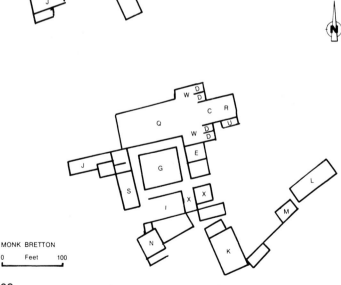

MONK BRETTON

0   Feet   100

MOUNT GRACE PRIORY

Founded in 1398, Mount Grace Priory, lying in quiet seclusion close to the A19 near Osmotherley, gives a unique opportunity for seeing the layout of a Carthusian monastery, for the ruins are more extensive than any other of the nine Carthusian houses in England.

The Carthusian Order, founded by St. Bruno at La Chartreuse in 1084, first settled at Witham in Surrey late in the twelfth century but the attraction of the Carthusian way of life did not make its impact until 1343. Between then and 1414 seven more charterhouses, as Carthusian monasteries came to be known, were built.

Founded by Thomas Holand, Duke of Surrey and Earl of Kent, nephew of Richard II, the House of the Assumption of the Most Blessed Virgin and St. Nicholas of Mount Grace in Ingleby, to give the priory its full title, was the eighth Carthusian monastery to be built in England and the only one in Yorkshire.

When Richard II was deposed, Thomas Holand lost his dukedom and after rebelling against Henry IV was beheaded at Cirencester. For a while the monks of Mount Grace were in trouble over their endowment but they survived and by the Dissolution, in December 1539, it ranked among the greater monasteries in wealth.

The history of Mount Grace is comparatively uneventful. Prior Wilson was suspected of playing a part in the Pilgrimage of Grace but nothing could be proved. He later joined the Carthusian house re-established at Shene when Mary was on the throne.

Prior Nicholas Love became noted for his translation, in the fifteenth century, of the Mirror of the Life of Christ, which was written by St. Bonaventure.

After the Dissolution the priory lands passed through a number of hands until they came to the Lascelles family in 1653. They converted the buildings on the north side of the gatehouse into a private residence and it remains

in use today while the rest of the monastery is in the hands of the National Trust. The property had come to the Bell family and when Sir Maurice Bell died the treasury accepted Mount Grace in lieu of death duties. The Treasury gave it to the National Trust who handed the ruins into the guardianship of the Ministry of Works, now the Department of the Environment.

The Carthusians, apart from living in seclusion from the world, had little contact with each other within the monastery. Each monk had a cell of his own where he worked, studied, ate, and slept. Each cell, provided with a garden, was completely cut off from its neighbours. This meant that the community was never as large as in monasteries where the monks slept in dormitories. At

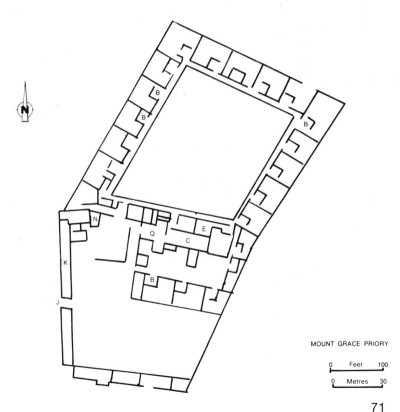

MOUNT GRACE PRIORY

0   Feet   100

0   Metres   30

Mount Grace twenty-four cells are easily traced and one has been reconstructed to show its original form.

Each cell was 27 ft. square with two storeys and adjoined the cloister wall in one corner of its garden. A doorway led on to the cloister from a small lobby which ran along the cloister wall and had a door into the garden. The rest of the ground floor was divided into three rooms, a bedroom and oratory, a study and a living room. The upper floor contained only one room used as a workshop. Food was brought to the monks in their cells and in order that the server and occupant should not see each other a special hatch, which made a right-angled bend, was constructed in the thickness of the wall. A garderobe was built in the outside garden wall.

The monks only ate together on Sundays and on certain feast days and came together in the church for morning High Mass, Vespers in the early afternoon and at midnight for Night Office.

The rest of the day was spent in manual labour, study and meditation, all within the confines of their own cell.

The monks were not allowed to speak to each other at any time except for a short period on Sunday afternoon, and during a walk outside the monastery once a week.

Barns, stables, and a guest house were arranged alongside the outer court and these were tended by lay-brothers who also did the kitchen work. No infirmary existed because when a monk was ill he was looked after in his own cell.

Because of the small numbers there was no need for a large frater, and the church was small and compact. The church was a plain rectangular building, 88 ft. by 25 ft., without aisles. Later two chapels were added, one on each side of the nave giving the plan the appearance of having transepts. To the east of these chapels two cross walls were built to carry a small tower separating the nave from the choir. The presbytery was added to the original church giving a total length of 118 ft. The chapel to the south of the presbytery has two altars and what is probably the base of a table tomb between them.

The cells are arranged around the large cloister on the north side of the church. At a later date a smaller one was brought into existence on the south side of the church to accommodate extra cells. This cloister was connected to the main one by a passage at the east side.

The range of building on the south side of the main cloister contain the rectangular chapter-house and at the west end the small frater, the remains of which indicate that at some time this room was reduced in size.

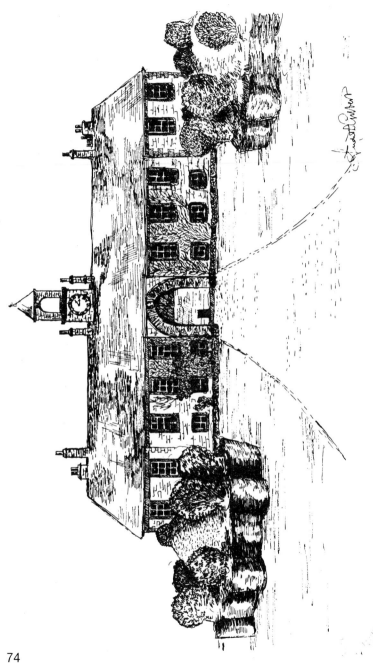

NEWBURGH PRIORY

Some monks from the Augustinian Priory at Bridlington, which had been founded in 1113, settled at Newburgh when Roger de Mowbray gave them land in 1145.

These monks, who are known as 'Augustinian Canons', 'The Regular Canons of St. Augustine', or 'Austin Canons', followed the Rule of St. Augustine of Hippo, which is not a detailed list of regulations, as is the Rule of St. Benedict, but is a short document of advice and suggestions with only a few regulations. The Augustinian houses adopted much from the way of life of the Benedictine monasteries but, being less severe, their life fell between that of the Benedictines and the easygoing way of the world outside the monasteries.

Although Newburgh never achieved the size or importance of Rievaulx or Byland, it prospered through generous donations, and at the Dissolution of the Monasteries it was wealthier than either of them. There is no evidence of any great upheaval, prolonged internal strife or important impact on the religious or national scene by the Newburgh monks. They merely got on with the monastic way of life which they had chosen, devoting their lives to God and playing their part in that particular strata of medieval society. One of the monks, known as William of Newburgh (1136-1201) was an historian and has been called the father of historical criticism particularly through his work Historia Rerum Angelicarum.

Newburgh was visited by Margaret Tudor for a night in July 1503 when she was on her way to Scotland to marry James IV. This was an important occasion for the monks, for among her retinue of over 200 people were some of the most important nobles in the land. As a commemoration, the monks built a fine Tudor porch with windows and columns rising to the top of the building. To the west of this is a section which contains the oldest part of the priory.

Content in their way of life and settled at Newburgh, the monks were reluctant to give up their beloved priory when the king determined to dissolve the monasteries. Rather than resist and incur the king's displeasure, the community felt, but only after the prior had laid a curse on a room which they were constructing. The room was not completed, and has remained unfinished to this day. Strange stories are told about the happenings there.

Unlike many of the monastic houses, Newburgh was not allowed to degenerate into a ruin. Henry gave it to his Chaplain, Dr. Anthony Bellasyse, one of the commissioners in charge of closing the monasteries. He passed it on to his nephew William, who saw the potential of the buildings for conversion into a country house. His plans resulted in a fine Elizabethan building set in beautiful gardens. William's grandson, Thomas, was created Earl Fauconberg by Charles I, and was succeeded by his grandson, also Thomas, whose second marriage was to Mary, daughter of Oliver Cromwell. This association gives rise to the speculation regarding the whereabouts of Cromwell's body.

Cromwell died a natural death in 1658 and was buried in Westminster Abbey. Charles II had the body exhumed and publicly beheaded. The head was displayed on a spike over Westminster Hall and, some time later, after it had blown down one stormy night, it was restored to the Cromwell family and eventually buried at Cambridge. But there are various stories as to what happened to the body.

One says that Cromwell's body rests in St. Nicholas' Church, Chiswick. In 1882 the vicar, the Rev. Lawford Dale, stated that his search for the body had proved unsuccessful, but some of his son's letters, found in 1969, indicate that his father deliberately concealed the fact that Cromwell was buried in the church vault.

Other stories say that Cromwell's body was buried at Tyburn, that it was thrown into the Thames and yet another that he was buried at Naseby where he had achieved a great victory.

Newburgh enters the story as it is said that Mary, Cromwell's daughter, had her father's body removed from Tyburn at dead of night and brought it north to Newburgh where it was placed in a special tomb within the house.

The two most likely resting places are Newburgh and Chiswick and it may be that the stories concerning both are partly right.

After Cromwell's natural death his heart would probably have been embalmed, as was the custom, and this is what Mary would bring to Newburgh, while the body after the beheading at Tyburn, would be disposed of quickly in a convenient place, St. Nicholas' Church, Chiswick, a church to which Lady Fauconberg had a long devotion.

Successive owners of Newburgh Priory have resisted the temptation to open the tomb as it was supposed to bring bad luck and even death to do so. Even the persuasion of King Edward VII, who stayed at Newburgh when he was Prince of Wales, was resisted.

The Newburgh estates passed by marriage to the Wombwell family in whose possession they remain today.

RIEVAULX ABBEY

Rievaulx Abbey, nestling in the valley of the Rye, five miles north of Helmsley, in what has been described as one of the most beautiful settings in Europe, was founded by Cistercian monks in 1131.

When St. Bernard, Abbot of Clairvaux, wanted other Cistercian monasteries to be established in England he sent his former secretary, William, with twelve monks, direct from Clairvaux to the north of England.

Walter Espec, Lord of Helmsley, gave them land beside the Rye.

Rievaulx's growth was rapid under William's guidance and after only eleven years there were 640 men dependent on the monastery, 140 of them monks, 240 were lay-brothers and 260 hired men.

However, Rievaulx's great and better known days came during the reign of St. Aelred, 1147 to 1167.

St. Aelred was born of a good Saxon family in Hexham about 1110. His father prevailed upon the Archbishop of York to re-establish the monastery at Hexham, which had been destroyed by the Danes. The two Augustinian Canons who came would be Aelred's first contact with the monastic way of life. Something of their influence must have remained with him and counter-acted the strong attractions of the high circles in which he moved.

Prince David of Scotland, whose sister was Queen to Henry I of England, married the daughter of a Saxon Earl of Northumberland. Wanting a companion for their son, Henry, they asked if Aelred might join their household. Permission was given and subsequently Aelred moved to the court of Scotland when David became king in 1124.

He became the confidant of both the king and his son, rising to a position of trust as Steward of the Royal Household. His future seemed mapped out for him, but contact with King David's stepson, Waltheof, who joined the Augustinian Canons at Kirkham, may have rekindled Aelred's attraction for the religious life.

In 1134, while visiting Archbishop Thurston at York on business, Aelred heard about the Cistercians at Rievaulx and, being interested in their life, visited their monastery. He joined the community and the talents which had been evident at court soon impressed Abbot William, who, after Aelred had served his novitiate, took him to Rome, and on their return to Rievaulx made him Novice-Master.

While expanding in its own right, Rievaulx was also fulfilling its purpose as a mission centre. Monks went to found monasteries in 1136 at Melrose, and Warden, and in 1142 at Dundrenna. In 1143 it was decided to establish a monastery under the patronage of William, Earl of Lincoln, at Revesby. Aelred was appointed abbot, and with twelve monks settled in Lincolnshire.

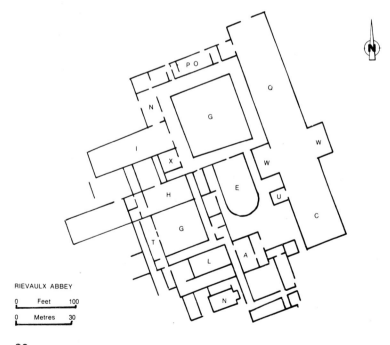

RIEVAULX ABBEY

0 Feet 100

0 Metres 30

On Abbot William's death in 1145, Maurice was elected abbot but his reign was shortlived, for he found the responsibilities of ruling over a large monastery were detracting from the spiritual life he was so anxious to follow. He resigned and, in 1147, Aelred became Abbot of Rievaulx. Abbot William had laid a solid foundation and Aelred built on it, both materially and spiritually, and for a period he was head of the Cistercian order in England. He was a wise councellor and leader, a man in touch with the affairs of the time, and above all a spiritual example to his fellow monks.

He was only 57 when he died after suffering from arthritis and a kidney complaint for ten years. Though often in pain, he still continued to fulfil his functions as abbot until shortly before his death on 12 January 1167.

The River Rye flowed much nearer the east side of the valley than it does now, and it also formed the boundary between Espec's lands and those of Roger de Mowbray. So, on the available land, the church could not be built on the traditional east-west axis and had to be erected on a roughly north-south orientation.

Later the Rievaulx monks sought permission from Roger de Mowbray to alter the course of the river and still keep it as a boundary between the two estates. He agreed, thus giving more land to the Rievaulx community, and later two further agreements resulted in the diversion of the river to the west side of the valley.

An abbey, especially of the size and importance of Rievaulx, exerted wide-ranging influences. The monks were first and foremost men of religion and their spiritual outlook must have helped the spread of Christian ideals. But in many other ways they influenced the life of the neighbourhood.

According to their rule, the Cistercians were expected to be self-supporting in the matter of food. As the monastery grew this meant that more and more land was needed to meet their requirements. Rievaulx was fortunate in its

82

benefactors, and grants of land were made, not only in the vicinity of the monastery but also in Bilsdale, the Vale of Mowbray, Ryedale and the Vale of Pickering. Such scattered lands could not all be worked from the monastery so a group of buildings, known as a grange, were built on each site and lay-brothers lived there, returning to the parent house on special occasions, or moving to other granges rather than reside permanently in one.

Sheep farming was important to the Rievaulx monks and at one time they owned 14,000 sheep. After the early days of buying fish at Teesmouth and Scarborough the monks followed the rule of self-support and established a fishery of their own at Teesmouth. They were always looking for the opportunity to develop available resources, and opened iron mines in Bilsdale and as far away as Wakefield.

Stone for the building of the monastery was quarried locally, in Hollins Wood, about a mile south of the abbey, and near Bow Bridge in the opposite direction. In order to transport the stone from the quarries to the building site the monks dug canals from the river. These are probably the oldest industrial canals known in England. Bow Bridge is about a mile from the abbey and the canal, which was cut close to the bottom of the hill, received its water by damming the Rye at Penny Piece Quarry, so called because the quarrymen were said to receive a penny a day for their labours. The stone so transported was used in the early church built on the highest part of the site about 200 yards from the canal. The stone was probably hauled to the site by cart or sled either before or after it was dressed.

There are still signs of groove-marks on the hillside from Hollins Wood quarry to the canal, showing that sleds were used for this part of the operation. Because the ground rises from the site of the dam, providing water for this canal, towards the abbey, the canal must have had a lock, probably a staunch or flushlock, though no evidence of it remains.

Rievaulx became known throughout England and in the religious centres of Europe as far as Rome, but its progress was not always smooth. Weather and disease played havoc with the sheep flocks and on two occasions the abbey was bankrupt. Maurauding Scots looted and pillaged the area a number of times. Few places escaped the dreaded Black Death of 1349-50 and the community of Rievaulx must have suffered. The mention of lay-brothers becomes less and less frequent and in 1380 there were only 18. At the Dissolution in 1536 there were only 24 monks and Rievaulx was left to fall into ruins and remain a memorial to the monks who lived there in peace, serving God and exerting their influence quietly on the neighbouring countryside for 400 years.

The oldest parts of the buildings are in the church, the nave and parts of the transepts, erected between 1135-40. The plain severe character of this work is typical of the early Cistercian buildings, in which the criteria were adequacy and dignity, without being ornate.

As the number of monks increased, an aisled choir and presbytery were added in the thirteenth century. Five more chapels were built at the end, adding to those already in the transepts and nave. By this time the Cistercians were overlooking the plain nature of their early work, and, building with some flair and imagination, left their impression on the architectural developments of the time.

They were enthusiastic builders, but everything had to serve a purpose. There was no building for building's sake but there was a new delight and freedom in their work. The Burgundian ideas which influenced their early work were supplanted by a natural development within England. The ground plan was related to elevation, and triforium and clerestory became evident. These, coupled with beautiful designs in ornament and moulding, ribbed stone-vaulting, with fine and imaginative treatment in other aspects of the church, made Rievaulx an outstanding example of the beautiful English Gothic style.

Five arches in the cloister have been reconstructed from original pieces showing the fine arcade of round headed arches which formed the cloister walk of the late twelfth century. Here monks walked, taking exercise while praying or reading.

Instead of the usual vaulted, rectangular building of the Cistercian chapter-house there is an oblong room with an apse, following the Benedictine plan. The seats for the monks are set against an arcade which encloses the room, and behind which there is an aisle. This aisle was vaulted, but the actual chapter-house had a flat ceiling for the height of the floor above in relation to the width of the room was not sufficient to allow for stone vaulting. Abbots used to be buried in the chapter-house, and three gravestones remain, those of William Panchard, 6th Abbot, Peter, 20th Abbot, and John, 22nd Abbot.

In the wall of the chapter-house are the remains of what was once an elaborate shrine. Two inscriptions relating to this refer to St. William and indicate that his coffin laid there. But there is nothing to mark the exact resting place of St. Aelred. There is an empty coffin in the middle of the chapter-house, and, as Aelred was a man of great importance, this could possibly have been his tomb.

Between the chapter-house and the church was a vestry and library while on the other side was the parlour and next to that the treasury. The parlour was the only place where the monks were allowed to converse, and the treasury housed anything of value.

The warming house, a room in which a fire was kept burning for the comfort of the community, the frater and kitchen were built during a reconstruction programme in the early thirteenth century. The frater stands on top of a vaulted undercroft, unusual in Cistercian abbeys, but here use was made of the fall of the land. The undercroft possibly served as a storage place, but it had the unusual feature of two fireplaces, so part of it may have been used by the novices. At meal times the monks were read to, and a pulpit for the reader was built on one side of the frater with access by stairs built into the wall.

The lay-brother's range which runs from the nave to the kitchen was built in the twelfth century but seems small and inadequate for the number of lay-brothers attached to the monastery, though in time many of them were using Rievaulx's various granges.

The infirmary was originally built in the twelfth century but the large building underwent various reconstructions and alterations. Wooden partitions between small rooms were replaced by stone walls and extra fireplaces were added in the fourteenth and fifteenth centuries. But the biggest change to these buildings came early in the sixteenth century when they were redesigned to serve as a residence for the abbot.

These old stones, forming one of the most beautiful ruined abbeys in England, heard the tread of monks feet again in 1967 when Benedictine and Cistercian monks

took part in a service held in the ruins to commemorate
the six-hundredth anniversary of the death of St. Aelred.

ROCHE ABBEY

The approach to Roche Abbey is through an impressive gatehouse in which much of the fine vaulting of the lower storey remains. It is overshadowed by white limestone cliffs of a narrow valley which opens into a spacious amphitheatre bounded by tree-lined slopes.

Cistercian monks made good use of the site and the abbey seems to snuggle comfortably in what must have been a very secluded spot.

Dedicated to St. Mary, as was the custom of the Cistercians, Roche Abbey presents one of the best layouts of an abbey in the country.

Though only the chancel and transepts remain to any great height, careful excavation and preservation have revealed every other part of the monastery.

These buildings follow the usual twelfth century Cistercian plan. The oldest part is the west range dating from the late twelfth century. This was the lay-brothers' frater with dorter over and gave the monks accommodation while they were building the abbey. The monks' frater in the south range ran north-south and parallelled the monks' dorter in the east range. Their length carried them both over the fast flowing stream which acted as the monastery's drain. Above this and running at right angles to the monks' dorter was their reredorter.

That these buildings extended on to the south bank of the stream, where there were also the lay-brothers' infirmary, abbot's kitchen, abbot's lodging and infirmarian's lodging, was due to the generosity of two benefactors.

When the Cistercians came here in 1147 from Newminster in Northumberland, which had been established from Fountains, Richard Fitz Turgis and Richard de Bully gave them adjacent land from their estates on either side of the stream.

Like other abbeys its fortunes waxed and waned.

The twenty monks and sixty lay-brothers living there shortly after its foundation had dwindled to fourteen monks and one lay-brother by the late fourteenth century. When it fell to the King in 1538 there were nineteen monks in residence.

The church was completed by 1170 and had a short chancel. The short transepts each held two chapels. This section, while showing the simplicity of the Cistercian view towards their churches, demonstrates the move away from the massive forms which had dominated the architectural scene. Here the pointed arch is starting to come into its own. Decoration no longer forms an aesthetic purpose only but is beginning to be an integral part of the construction. The whole eventually took on a flowing, lighter look. The early development of this appears at Roche while there remains the solid, massive pre-Gothic features.

That there is not more of the church to study for architectural developments is due to local people who plundered the buildings after the Dissolution.

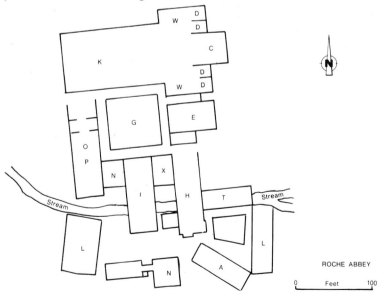

ROCHE ABBEY

0   Feet   100

91

SAWLEY ABBEY

Approximately three miles from Clitheroe and on the eastern bank of the River Ribble stands what used to be known as Yorkshire's unluckiest monastery. It suffered at the hands of the raiding Scots in the fourteenth century. A series of poor harvests almost brought a decision to abandon the abbey but endowments from the Percy family saved the situation. A quarrel over trading competition with the monks who had established a monastery at Whalley in 1296 was not settled until the Cistercian General Chapter in 1305.

Sawley Abbey was founded in 1147 by William, Baron Perci, grandson of William de Perci who accompanied the Conqueror to England. Thirteen monks and ten lay-brothers came from Newminster in Northumberland to establish what was to become, in spite of the difficulties, a monastery renowned for its learning. Among its writers was Abbot Stephen (1224-1233), a spiritual writer, and Prior William became Chancellor of Oxford University (1372-1373).

The abbey was suppressed in 1536 but twenty-one monks were reinstated during the Pilgrimage of Grace by the insurgents. This laid them open to the anger of the King. They were expelled a second time and their abbot, William Trafford, was executed on 10 March 1537.

Though there is little left but the foundations the lay-out of the abbey can be seen clearly. The highest part of the stonework is the south-west angle of the nave. The aisled chancel is much broader and longer (116 ft.) than the aisled nave which is usually short (40 ft.). This came about because the better proportioned original church was shortened, early in the sixteenth century, by the building of a wall across the nave. When the chancel was extended and broadened it was decided that the western part of the nave was superflous to the needs of the community.

Little remains of the claustral buildings which followed the usual Cistercian pattern. The lay-brothers' quarters in the west range were converted into the abbot's lodgings when the number of lay-brothers had dropped to a point where a large building was no longer required for their needs.

Extensive excavations took place in 1848, uncovering the floors of the church, cloister and chapter-house. A stone coffin was unearthed, the only one to be found in the abbey precincts. On its lid was carved a pair of shears indicating that it was the tomb of a lady. There was no clue as to who she was.

There are many stones placed on one side at the entrance to the abbey, some of which have interesting carvings. The two fine arches across the road were created with materials recovered during the excavations.

94

SELBY ABBEY

Although nothing remains of the claustral buildings the fine church bears witness to the great abbey which once occupied an important position in the life of Selby and the surrounding countryside.

It is precisely because of this role that the church remained intact at the Dissolution of the Monasteries while the rest of the abbey, devoid of monks, fell into disuse and eventually disappeared altogether.

The monastery was founded by Benedictines on a site close to a small gathering of people. Unlike some communities the Benedictines did not cut themselves off from everyday life and in the case of Selby their church became the place of worship for the local people.

Although the monks were turned out of their monastery at the Dissolution, the townspeople still required a place to worship and so the church remained unspoiled, to continue in the function for which it had been built, though it did not legally become a parish church until 1618.

The foundation of Selby Abbey came about through two men, vastly different in character and in their station in life – King William I, the Conqueror, and Benedict, a monk of Auxerre in France.

The story goes that Benedict had a vision of St. Germain, who as Bishop of Auxerre was sent by the Pope in 429 and again in 447 to put down the Pelagian heresy in Britain. Guided by his vision, Benedict left his monastery and came to Britain in 1069. Seeking the scene of his vision he took a ship bound for York from Kings Lynn, but at Selby he found what he was looking for. Disembarking he took the sight of three swans alighting on the river as a sign that the Holy Trinity confirmed his belief. Three swans appear on Selby Abbey's coat of arms.

The small religious community which was established beside the tiny settlement of lay-folk came to the notice of Hugh, Sheriff of York. He offered the monks help and, because they were on royal ground, took Benedict to meet King William who was in York after putting down insurrection in the north.

William regarded himself as champion of the Church and saw the advantage of linking this with political aspirations. The founding of an abbey in this part of the country would not only show his tolerance and generosity but it would influence the district in its loyalty to him. Accordingly he granted the monks land at Selby with permission to build a monastery on it and Benedict became its first abbot.

The building of the church started in 1100 under Abbot Hugh. The stone was brought from Monk Fryston, eight miles away, on a canal especially constructed for this purpose. The choir was less than half the length of the present one which is 140 ft. Nothing of that first choir is left but it is known that it was apsidal as also were the chapels at the east side of the two transepts which were completed about the same time. Although the entire nave was envisaged it was not completed during Hugh's term

as abbot. Massive round pillars support graceful round arches, solid in strength that not even the sinking of the tower foundation about the mid-twelfth century could upset them completely, though distortion can be seen in the easternmost arch. One particularly fine pillar is decorated with a trellis pattern and is known as Abbot Hugh's pillar.

As the nave was built from east to west it shows the various stages in the development of English architecture over 130 years. The simplicity of the early Norman pillars and arches gives way to lighter style with delicate mouldings so that by about 1170 when the desired length was reached the Norman period of architecture had given way to the Transitional. By the time the treforium was completed the architectural development had moved into the Early English period with its pointed arches.

The west front with squat towers and the clerestory took the church which Abbot Hugh had visualised to its completion by about 1230.

With the growth of monastic numbers and of wealth, it was decided to build a bigger choir. Accordingly the east end of the new choir was the first part to be built, so that the choir could progress westwards without interfering with the existing choir until it was almost completely enclosed by the new. This period of building, 1280-1340, saw the introduction of much lighter work with fine traceried windows. Particularly notable is the east window. Though a great deal of the glass had to be restored there is still sufficient of the old to capture the fourteenth century magnificence of the seven, tall, slender lights, the stonework of which leads up to a swirl of beautiful tracery. What is now the War Memorial Chapel, built out on the south side of the choir, was erected in the same period. It was originally the sacristy with scriptorium above.

The window above the west door and that at the end of the north transept are fifteenth century with glass of a later date. That in the north transept is early twentieth century almost overwhelming in the detail of the facts and legends of St. Germain, to whom the church is dedicated along with Our Lord and St. Mary.

Also of the fifteenth century is the chapel on the east side of the north transept now used as a vestry. Here is a squint cut through seven feet of masonry. Some say that it was to enable lepers to watch the altar from outside but squints were generally inserted in side chapels so that the priest saying Mass there could also observe the service at the High Altar so that his elevation of the Host did not clash with that of the main service.

Although the church escaped destruction at the Dissolution it suffered badly at the hands of the Parliamentarians during the Civil War (1642-1651). They destroyed the statues and broke the fine glass in the north transept.

The church fell into disrepair and when the central tower collapsed it destroyed the south aisle in 1690. A wall was built across the chancel and the choir was used for services while the nave served as a warehouse. This wall was removed at the end of the nineteenth century in the wake of some tidying up and some restoration work.

On 19 October 1906 a fire raged through the church and it was feared it would be completely destroyed. After the conflagration, however, careful examination revealed that a great deal of stonework had not been affected. Restoration was possible. This was undertaken immediately and at a brisk pace. A year later the nave was finished and by 1909 the choir and the tower were complete. The south transept was restored in 1912. In 1935 the west front was altered by heightening the squat twin towers with an upper stage and replacing the original pinnacles on the new work.

Although a great deal of the work to be seen in Selby Abbey is of modern construction it has been so well done and blended so truely with the original that we still get the feel of the magnificence of medieval Selby.

98

WHITBY ABBEY

Christian and pagan forces were in military conflict during the seventh century. Edwin, King of Northumbria was defeated by a rebellious heathen chief, Cadwella, in 633 but in the following year revenge was exacted by Edwin's successor Oswald. A period of peace looked certain, and Oswald persuaded Aidan, a monk of Iona, to establish a monastery on the island of Lindisfarne in 635.

Penda of Mercia killed Oswald in battle in 642, and it was not until thirteen years later that Oswald's successor, his brother Oswy, finally defeated the pagan forces at Winwaed, near Leeds, and established Christianity in the country.

As a thanksgiving, King Oswy offered his daughter Aelfleda to the religious life and gave land for the establishment of monasteries. Aelfleda was sent to the monastery at Hartlepool where Hilda was abbess.

Hilda was born in 614, and at the age of thirteen was baptised with her great uncle, King Edwin, by Paulinus at York. She became a nun when she was thirty-three, and under the direction of Aidan founded a monastery at Monkwearmouth, but shortly after became abbess at Hartlepool where Aidan had established the first convent of nuns in England.

In 657 Hilda, bringing Aelfleda with her, came to Whitby, to land given by King Oswy, and founded what was to become an important monastery in the early church. Such was its reputation that it was chosen as the place to hold a synod in 664.

St. Augustine and his missionaries brought Christianity to the south of Britain and before long two streams of Christian traditions confronted each other, that of the Celtic monks from Scotland and Ireland, and that of the Benedictine monks from Gaul and Italy. At the Synod of Whitby which was convened to try to reconcile the differences, the followers of the Celtic traditions gave

way, so that one Christian view point was held throughout the country.

This Saxon monastery, high on the Yorkshire cliffs, consisting of two establishments one for men and one for women, both ruled over by Hilda, attracted many people to its walls. First and foremost it was a religious house, devoted to the praise and service of God, but it was also a place of education, and a self-supporting abbey so that there were a large number of lay-brethren, helpers and craftsmen.

Its reputation reached into Europe. Among the dignitaries who were trained there were Bosa and Wilfrid II, both of whom became Bishops of York, Aetla, Bishop of Dorchester, John, Bishop of Hexham, Tatfrid and Oftfor, Bishops of Worcester, and John of Beverley.

In the abbey church of St. Peter were buried Aelfleda, her mother Queen Eanfleda, King Oswy and King Edwin.

It was here that the birth of English Literature came about. A man appeared in a dream to Caedmon, an uneducated herdsman, telling him to sing. He said he was not able to do so, but the man persuaded him to try, and to take as his subject the beginning of created things. Caedmon did so, and when he woke in the morning, he remembered it all. He told his superior, who took him to see abbess Hilda. She recognised the work of God in the incident and admitted Caedmon to the monastery to learn the events of sacred history. These he set down in song and verse, the first in the English tongue.

Hilda died in 680 and was succeeded by Aelfleda who was abbess for thirty-four years. After her death, little is known about the abbey, but the Danes destroyed it in 866.

Among the Normans harrying the north was one called Reinfrid, who was moved to join a religious community and was admitted to that at Evesham. Four years later he, with Aldwin and Aelfwig, left for the north and settled at Jarrow. Reinfrid left there to establish a monastery on the site of the old one at Whitby, in 1076.

William de Percy, whose family were to become very powerful in the north, gave the land to Reinfrid and soon he was joined by other men. Shortly afterwards, due to some internal differences, Stephen and a small band of monks left to try to establish a monastery on the site of St. Cedd's monastery at Lastingham, but continued harrassment by robbers caused them to leave Lastingham in 1086 for York where two years later they formally founded St. Mary's Abbey.

William de Percy's brother, Serlo, became prior of the Benedictine priory of St. Peter and St. Hilda at Whitby. It was under his rule that the Norman church, the outline of which is still clearly visible among the present ruins, was started. The priory was raised to the status of an abbey and William, a nephew of Serlo, became its first abbot in 1089.

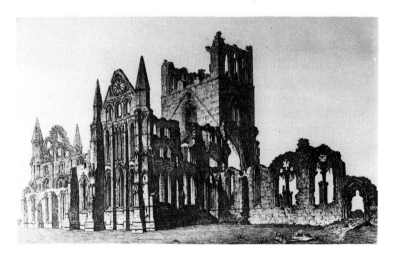

It is probable that the church and monastic buildings were completed before Abbot William's death in 1129. He was also responsible for building a leper hospital at Spittal Bridge and the parish church of St. Mary a short distance outside the abbey grounds. There seems to have been little of importance in the history of this second monastery. The monks went quietly about their way of life following the Rule of St. Benedict with only some internal minor upsets to disturb their peace.

Stripped of its lead, glass and valuables at the Dissolution on 14 December 1539, the abbey was left to crumble into ruin, but the church seems to have been fairly intact until 1711. After that its decay was more rapid. The nave fell in 1762 and the south transept the following year. In November 1794 most of the west front came down, but the greatest fall occurred on 25 June 1830 when the massive central tower came crashing to the ground. A German battle cruiser shelled Whitby on 16 December 1914 and the abbey gateway and west wall of the nave were hit. During all this time, as occurred at most other ruined abbeys, local people took stone from the ruins to build cottages and make roads, until the Ministry of Works took over in 1920.

From the ruins that remain it can be seen that Whitby Abbey was one of the finest examples of thirteenth century work in the country.

The rebuilding of the abbey church was begun about 1220, with the presbytery and its aisles, the north and south transepts, what was the central tower and part of the nave all belonging to the thirteenth century.

This building superceded the earlier one which had followed the Benedictine plan of having an apsidal east end. This can be seen clearly traced in the ground of the later presbytery.

The fine east end of the thirteenth century building shows the new thinking which had come into the building of churches in doing away with the apse and replacing it with a straight wall, in this case terminating without any projections at the edge of the aisles, which were carried straight through on either side of the presbytery.

The three tiers of fine lancet windows in this east wall must have shed a rare beauty along the length of the church when the early morning sunlight flooded through the stained glass. On the outside, tall, straight buttresses are capped with pinnacles while the gable end of the wall is flanked by octagonal turrets.

The same arrangement can be seen in the north wall of the north transept, though here the buttresses are topped with canopied niches and the three tiers of lancet windows are capped by an exquisite traceried round window.

The magnificent proportions of Whitby Abbey are experienced in the north transept most of which still stands to its full height. The arcade here reflects the fine arcade, with triforium and clerestory, of the presbytery where the north aisle shows some good ribbed vaulting.

Apart from the three bays near the central crossing, the nave was built in the fourteenth century as was the west end with its main doorway. We know from an aquatint of 1789 that this had a central pier dividing two openings each with a trefoiled head, the whole being surmounted by a large fifteenth century window.

Little remains of the domestic buildings but they stood to the south of the church with the cloister on the south side of the nave and the chapter-house at the end of the south transept.

Evidence of several small buildings has been found to the north of the present ruin. These may have been cells occupied by the inmates and as loom weights and toilet objects were found here these cells could have been the living quarters of the nuns, a supposition supported by the general fact that in double Saxon monasteries the nuns occupied the north side of the central longitudinal partition.

YORK, ST. MARY'S ABBEY

The light of monasticism which had shone brightly in the seventh and eighth centuries had been extinguished by the marauding Danes and the abbeys of the north lay in ruins.

In 1074 Aldwin, Reinfrid and Aelfwig, monks of the Saxon monastery at Evesham, journeyed north to Jarrow, famed for its associations with the Venerable Bede. From there Reinfrid went to the site of the old monastery high on the windswept cliffs above Whitby, where other men joined him.

Due to internal disputes in 1078 Stephen and a few monks left Whitby for the site of the former monastery of St. Cedd at Lastingham. Here they remained for eight years until the continual harrassment by robbers became so intolerable that they left to seek the safety of York.

Here they were given some land close to the city walls and a church dedicated to St. Olaf of Norway. When William Rufus visited York he found that the monks were in very poor circumstances and that their land was being claimed by the Archbishop of York. The king ruled in favour of the newcomers and took them under his Royal patronage, "......and seeing the building was too straight and narrow for us, he projected a larger; and with his own hand first opened the ground for laying the foundation of the church of the monastery." So St. Mary's Abbey came into being in 1088.

It prospered under Abbot Stephen's rule of twenty years (d. 1112) but with prosperity came some slackness in interpreting the Rule of St. Benedict. There were monks who sought perfection and in 1132 pressed their abbot, Geoffrey, for reform. This cry for reform mirrored in its small way the great reform which was sweeping through monasticism in Western Europe giving rise to other orders especially the Cistercians. These white monks were already in Yorkshire attracting the attention of those who sought a stricter way of life, with the old emphasis on prayer and work.

The matter within St. Mary's was discussed and held in abeyance for consideration. Prior Richard, wanting to get the matter settled, appealed to Archbishop Thurstan who agreed to a hearing before himself and the Abbot. At this point there was no thought of a real breakaway, but it came about when the Abbot refused to admit the Archbishop's supporters and attendants to the hearing. The Archbishop saw it as a challenge to his authority, and the reformers were given permission to leave St. Mary's. They lived with Archbishop Thurston for three months until just after Christmas in 1132, when the Archbishop gave them the present site of Fountains Abbey. If the Abbot and Archbishop had not differed, a peaceful solution may well have been found within the walls of St. Mary's Abbey itself.

As it was, the great monastery of Fountains came into being, and from there several other abbeys were

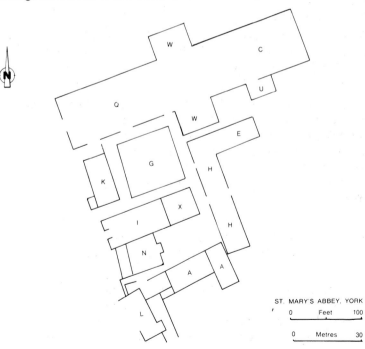

ST. MARY'S ABBEY, YORK

0   Feet   100

0   Metres   30

established. Fountains had come about through St. Mary's Abbey, York, which had been established from Whitby, which in turn had come from the old monastery at Evesham. The ripples sent out by the three Evesham monks journeying north had had far reaching consequences.

In spite of losing thirteen monks, St. Mary's continued to prosper and this must have been due in no small way to the guidance of its abbot and the attraction of the way of life led by the Benedictines there. Less than three years after the disagreement the abbot was able to approve the setting up of a daughter house at Lincoln with a prior and twelve monks, and in the following year the same number to Romburgh in Cambridgeshire.

St. Mary's grew in importance and survived conflicts with the city, and a fire in 1137. Although the damage by the fire is thought to have been extensive, the buildings continued to be used for another 133 years. When some of them became unsafe, reconstruction took place in the reign of Abbot Simon (1258-96), who was motivated by the desire to have a church befitting the high position St. Mary's held among the Benedictine Abbeys in England.

Building, which was begun in 1270, the twelfth year of his abbacy, took twenty-two years to complete and Abbot Simon not only lived to see the finished work, but also to celebrate Mass at its altars for another three years before he died. It is the ruins of his abbey which remain within the grounds of the Museum Gardens in York today.

During Abbot Simon's time, St. Mary's was made one of the two mitred abbeys in the north, the other being Selby. This meant that the abbot could be summoned to Parliament.

Its main function of following the religious way of life according to the Rule of St. Benedict seems to have been particularly successful, for at the Dissolution on 29 November 1539, there were 51 monks, a considerable number, especially when the figures for other northern abbeys are considered, Durham 28, Selby 23, Rievaulx 22 and Fountains 32.

With the abbey falling into ruin, stone was taken for a number of purposes, in 1566 to rebuild the centre of Ouse Bridge, in 1705 to repair damage done to St. Olave's Church during the Civil War, and in 1717 to repair parts of Beverley Minster. But early in the nineteenth century moves to preserve the ruins, before they were lost to the city found support, and restoration was put into action. For his work in this connection Samuel Sharp was awarded the Sloane medal in 1838.

It is unfortunate that so little remains of what must have been fine, impressive buildings of this leading and influential monastery.

The ruins standing today are of the second church, rebuilt between 1270 and 1294. They show the thinking which was taking place in church architecture resulting in this transitional stage between the Early English of the thirteenth century and the Decorated of the fourteenth century.

The section of the wall of the north aisle shows that the windows of two and three lights alternated with each other and all had geometric tracery. The south west pier of the central tower still stands as does part of the west end of the nave. Only a few other fragments remain and knowledge of the great abbey's appearance in both its church and domestic buildings comes largely through documentary evidence and excavations.

A cloister lay to the south of the nave as was usual, and beyond that was the frater and warming house. The south transept let into a vestibule which gave access to the rectangular chapter-house lying to the east and to the parlour with dormitory above to the south. This vestibule was in all probability the original chapter-house and was converted to its final use when the rebuilding took place.

Excavations in 1828 revealed several life-size figures along with a series of carved stones depicting biblical scenes. There are various schools of thought about the position they occupied but there is general agreement that they date from about 1200 and are in the transitional period between Romanesque and Gothic styles of figure sculpture.

Some say that they originally adorned the outside of the west front of the church, positioned against the shafts, while the slabs of biblical scenes adorned the niches. If this is so then this arrangement is important as the only attempt in England to imitate the doorways of this period in France.

Another opinion puts the statues in the vestibule and chapter-house with the forerunners of Christ occupying the vestibule through the twelve apostles on the chapter-house walls to Christ in majesty at the east end.

Whichever theory is correct the statues and carvings are unique. They are preserved in the Yorkshire Museum which stands in the abbey grounds close to the site the statues occupied seven centuries ago.

TIME CHART

Monastery	300 A.D.	400 A.D.	500 A.D.	600 A.D.	700 A.D.	800 A.D.	900 A.D.	1000 A.D.	1100 A.D.	1200 A.D.	1300 A.D.	1400 A.D.	1500 A.D.	1600 A.D.	1700 A.D.	1800 A.D.	1900 A.D.
BOLTON									█	█	█	█	█				
BYLAND									█	█	█	█	█				
EASBY									█	█	█	█	█				
EGGLESTONE										█	█	█	█				
FOUNTAINS									█	█	█	█	█				
GUISBOROUGH									█	█	█	█	█				
JERVAULX									█	█	█	█	█				
KIRKHAM									█	█	█	█	█				
KIRKSTALL									█	█	█	█	█				
LASTINGHAM		▪	▪				▪										
MALTON									█	█	█	█	█				
MONK BRETTON								█	█	█	█	█	█				
MOUNT GRACE												█					
NEWBURGH									█	█	█	█	█				
RIEVAULX									█	█	█	█	█				
ROCHE									█	█	█	█	█				
SAWLEY									█	█	█	█	█				
SELBY								█	█	█	█	█	█				
WHITBY				█	█			█	█	█	█	█	█				
YORK								█	█	█	█	█	█				

Complete List of the Medieval Monasteries of Yorkshire with page references.

Abbreviations: CR—considerable remains, FR—few remains, NR—no remains, PC—part of parish church, PH—part of private house.
C—Cleveland, D—Durham, H—Humberside, NY—North Yorkshire, SY—South Yorkshire, WY—West Yorkshire, L—Lancashire.

Monastery	Order	Rank	Dates	Remains	Location	Page
Arden	Benedictine Nuns	Priory	1147-1536	NR	NY	
Arthington	Cluniac Nuns	Priory	1154-1539	NR	WY	
Barnoldswick	Cistercian	Abbey	1147-1152	NR	L	
Baysdale	Cistercian Nuns	Priory	1189-1539	NR	NY	
Beauchief	Premonstratensian	Abbey	1175-1537	FR	SY	
Beverley	Dominican	Friary	1240-1539	FR	H	
Beverley	Franciscan	Friary	1267-1539	NR	H	
Bolton	Augustinian	Priory	1154-1540	CR	NY	24
Bridlington	Augustinian	Priory	1113-1537	PC	H	
Byland	Cistercian	Abbey	1177-1539	CR	NY	27
Cottingham	Augustinian	Priory	1322-1326	NR	H	
Coverham	Premonstratensian	Abbey	1202-1536	FR	NY	
Doncaster	Carmelite	Friary	1351-1538	NR	SY	
Doncaster	Franciscan	Friary	1284-1538	NR	SY	
Drax	Augustinian	Priory	1130-1535	NR	NY	
Easby	Premonstratensian	Abbey	1152-1537	CR	NY	32

Name	Order	Type	Dates			
Egglestone	Premonstratensian	Abbey	1195-1540	CR	D	36
Ellerton	Cistercian Nuns	Priory	1189-1537	FR	NY	
Ellerton	Gilbertine Canons	Priory	1207-1538	NR	NY	
Embsay	Augustinian	Priory	1120-1154	NR	NY	
Esholt	Cistercian Nuns	Priory	11 -1539	NR	NY	
Fors	Cistercian	Abbey	1145-1156	NR	NY	
Foukeholme	Benedictine Nuns	Priory	1199-1349	NR	NY	
Fountains	Cistercian	Abbey	1132-1539	CR	NY	
Grosmont	Grandmontine	Priory	1204-1536	NR	NY	40
Guisborough	Augustinian	Priory	1119-1540	CR	C	46
Hackness	Benedictine	Cell	1095-1539	NR	NY	
Haltemprice	Augustinian	Priory	1326-1536	NR	H	
Hampole	Cistercian Nuns	Priory	1156-1539	NR	NY	
Handale	Cistercian Nuns	Priory	1137-1539	NR	C	
Healaugh	Augustinian	Priory	1218-1535	FR	NY	
Hood	Cistercian	Abbey	1138-1143	NR	NY	
Hood	Augustinian	Priory	1143-1145	NR	NY	
Hood	Augustinian	Cell	1145-1539	NR	NY	
Hutton	Cistercian	Priory	1162-1167	NR	C	
Jervaulx	Cistercian	Abbey	1156-1537	CR	NY	48
Keldholm	Cistercian Nuns	Priory	1135-1535	NR	NY	
Kildale	Crutched	Friary	1310-1313	NR	NY	
Kingston-upon-Hull	Carmelite	Friary	1290-1539	NR	H	

113

Name	Order	Type	Dates			
Kirkham	Augustinian	Priory	1122-1539	CR	NY	52
Kirkstall	Cistercian	Abbey	1152-1540	CR	WY	56
Kirklees	Cistercian Nuns	Priory	1138-1539	FR	WY	
Knaresborough	Trinitarian	Friary	1252-1538	NR	NY	
Lastingham	Benedictine	Abbey	1078-1086	PC	NY	60
Malton	Gilbertine	Priory	1150-1539	PC	NY	64
Marrick	Benedictine Nuns	Priory	1158-1540	FR	NY	
Marton	Augustinian Canons & Nuns	Priory	1154-1536	NR	NY	
Meaux	Cistercian	Abbey	1151-1539	NR	H	
Middlesbrough	Benedictine	Priory/Cell	1120-1537	NR	C	
Monk Bretton	Cluniac, later Benedictine	Priory	1154-1539	CR	SY	67
Mount Grace	Carthusian	Priory	1398-1539	CR	NY	69
Moxby	Benedictine Nuns & Augustinian Nuns	Priory	1167-1536	NR	NY	
Newburgh	Augustinian	Priory	1145-1538	PH	NY	74
Northallerton	Carmelite	Friary	1356-1538	NR	NY	
North Ferriby	Augustinian	Priory	1140-1536	NR	H	
Nostell	Augustinian	Priory	1120-1539	NR	NY	
Nun Appleton	Cistercian Nuns	Priory	1150-1539	NR	NY	
Nunburnholme	Benedictine Nuns	Priory	11 -1536	NR	NY	
Nunkeeling	Benedictine Nuns	Priory	1152-1539	NR	H	
Nun Monkton	Benedictine Nuns	Priory	1153-1536	FR	NY	

Location	Order	Type	Date			Page
Nunthorpe	Cistercian Nuns	Priory	1167-1189	NR	C	
Old Byland	Cistercian	Abbey	1143-1147	NR	NY	
Pontefract	Dominican	Friary	1256-1538	NR	WY	
Richmond	Benedictine	Priory	1100-1539	FR	NY	
Richmond	Franciscan	Friary	1258-1539	FR	NY	
Rievaulx	Cistercian	Abbey	1132-1538	CR	NY	78
Roche	Cistercian	Abbey	1147-1538	CR	SY	88
Rosedale	Cistercian Nuns	Priory	1158-1535	FR	NY	
Sawley	Cistercian	Abbey	1147-1536	CR	L	92
Scalby	Franciscan	Friary	1245-1270	NR	NY	
Scarborough	Dominican	Friary	1252-1539	NR	NY	
Selby	Benedictine	Abbey	1069-1539	PC	NY	94
Sinningthwaite	Cistercian Nuns	Priory	1160-1535	FR	NY	
Skewkirk	Augustinian	Cell	1114-1540	NR	NY	
Snaith	Benedictine	Priory/Cell	1310-1539	PC	H	
Stocking	Cistercian	Abbey	1147-1177	NR	NY	
Swainby	Premonstratensian	Abbey	1187-1202	NR	NY	
Swine	Cistercian	Priory	1153-1539	PC	H	
Thicket	Benedictine Nuns	Priory	1180-1539	NR	NY	
Tickhill	Augustinian	Friary	1256-1538	NR	SY	
Warter	Augustinian Nuns	Priory	1132-1536	NR	NY	
Watton	Gilbertine Nuns & Canons	Priory	1150-1539	PH	H	99
Whitby	Benedictine	Abbey	1077-1539	CR	NY	
Wilberfoss	Benedictine Nuns	Priory	1153-1539	NR	NY	

Woodkirk	Augustinian	Cell	1135-1539	NR	NY
Wykeham	Cistercian Nuns	Priory	1153-1539	FR	NY
Yarm	Dominican	Friary	1266-1538	NR	C
Yeddingham	Benedictine Nuns	Priory	1163-1539	FR	NY
York	Benedictine	Abbey	1086-1088	NR	NY
(first home of the monks who came from Lastingham and founded St. Mary's Abbey)					
York (Fishergate)	Benedictine	Priory	1087-1536	NR	NY
York (Micklegate. Some remains in parish church)	Benedictine	Priory	1089-1538	FR	NY
York (Clementhorpe)	Benedictine Nuns	Priory	1130-1536	NR	NY
York (Fishergate)	Gilbertine	Priory	1200-1538	NR	NY
York (Toft Green)	Dominican	Friary	1227-1538	NR	NY
York (Near Castle)	Franciscan	Friary	1230-1538	NR	NY
York (Bootham & Stonebow)	Carmelite	Friary	1253-1538	NR	NY
York	Sack Friars	Friary	1260-1312	NR	NY
York (Lendal)	Augustinian	Friary	1272-1538	NR	NY
York	Crutched	Friary	1307-1310	NR	NY
York (St. Mary's)	Benedictine	Abbey	1088-1539	CR	NY